IMPROVE WITH

IMPROV!

A Guide to Improvisation and Character Development

BRIE
JONES

MERIWETHER PUBLISHING LTD.
Colorado Springs, Colorado

Meriwether Publishing Ltd., Publisher
P.O. Box 7710
Colorado Springs, CO 80933

Editor: Theodore O. Zapel
Typesetting: Susan Trinko
Cover design: Tom Myers

© Copyright MCMXCIII Meriwether Publishing Ltd.
Printed in the United States of America
First Edition

Library of Congress Cataloging-in-Publication Data

Jones, Brie, 1928-
    Improve with improv! : a classroom guide to improvisation and character development / Brie Jones. -- 1st ed.
        p.   cm.
      ISBN 0-916260-98-4
      1. Improvisation (Acting)   I. Title
PN2071.I5J66   1993
792'.028--dc20
                                         93-24919
                                           CIP

4   5   6   7   8   9   03   02   01   00   99

*For all my students who risked
and brought me joy.*

"I always looked at theater as having an inner connection with the human condition. Therefore, you could learn things about yourself through acting. When you examine a character who goes through circumstances that cause rage, panic, despair, all these different emotions, you start to examine certain things inside yourself. It was always from this desire of trying to understand what the hell I'm doing here and what life is all about."

Nick Nolte
Actor

"Mastering improv makes all other forms of acting easier."

Mike Nichols
Director

CONTENTS

Introduction

Improvisation is an activity requiring performers to *think*. Improv is about life. It is about human behavior, conflicts and inner relationships. An understanding of these elements comes through the art of improv, where portraying a character brings out an awareness of self and of others. The same skills needed for improv are also useful for interesting living.

Improvisation will help students and community theatre actors expand their horizons. It can prepare beginners for any other type of dramatic work as well as keep professional actors alert and creative. And, it can bolster the self-concept of participants in senior-citizen workshops.

Taking on a role in improv stretches boundaries. It allows players to utilize their imagination. They are able to discover something of themselves and often transcend their everyday lives. All that is needed is an openness to experimentation and not being afraid to fail. Enough structure allows for success. In other learning activities, mistakes are *expected*. In bicycling you fall over, in skiing you fall down, in ballet you experience awkwardness. Why would actors have fewer expectations?

To risk on stage is to have fun!

Improv can be performed in any space available. A stage is preferable, but a large room can substitute. Furniture and props are not as important as the energy of the group. A few chairs, perhaps a bench or two, and a card table will suffice. Hand props can be supplied by both the instructor and students as needed.

Workshop guidelines I stress include the content and goal for the improvs. The content of presentations should not include material that is racist, political or religious. The goal is to be creative and clever, not raunchy.

1

Presented on the following pages are creative improv activities I used to motivate and stimulate acting students in a community college class. Some of the students were professional. Most were not. The format may be utilized with any and all age groups. Workshops are explained in detail as I have conducted them, but the form may be easily changed by any instructor. The same techniques, when modified, can be adjusted to different performers' requirements.

The degree of involvement sets the time limits. For a group of 30, I allowed a two-and-a-half-hour weekly session. Generally, an average of 25 students attended each class. If there were fewer players, I introduced all the exercises outlined.

Time limits for each individual or group activity I controlled with a warning bell if the performance was too long. Sometimes, if the bell did not have effect, I would throw a rubber chicken on-stage as a "get-off" reminder. Concept of *time* is an added learning experience in improv. Less is more!

At the beginning of improv instructions, I sometimes suggested that each actor assign himself an ongoing character trait to be used whenever he was performing an improvisation. Even though he was a different character in each week's improvs, the gimmick was reinforced through repetition and provided a subtext on which to base character development. For example, traits included tardiness, asthma attacks, fastidiousness, penny-pinching, bloody noses, forgetfulness, phobias or limps.

Although this is a teaching syllabus, with lecture notes supported by exercises, the purpose is not to supply the instructor with lesson plans that will require rigid conformity. For instance, with professional actors I schedule animal exercises, physicalization and pantomime sessions first because body language needs to come before verbalization.

But for young students or senior citizens, these really off-the-wall classes seem to be too challenging and risky. I found I lost some of my audience. Therefore, I offer physicalization near the beginning and pantomime and animals well into the program along with gibberish, commedia and other more esoteric subjects. By then, the actors are ready and eager to stretch and go where they have never been before.

The activities here are a point of departure, exercises from which a teacher's creative mind can further invent. After a while, the instructor's own style and point of view may flow from these ideas.

The enjoyment the leader can derive from directing improv is incalculable.

(Note: I refer to all players as "he" to simplify the work.)

Chapter 1
ORIENTATION

Icebreaker

As a new class meets for the first time, it may be useful to hand out cards with instructions such as:

— Find a person who has Morton's toe (the fourth toe is longer than the big toe).

— Find a person who has the same-sized thumb as you do.

— Find a person who likes broccoli.

— Find a person who can titter.

Or, a different set of cards can be passed out directing each student to ask someone a question, such as:

— "If you could change your age, what age would you rather be?"

— "What part of a parade would you like to be?"

— "What is your definition of success?"

There is no discussion of these cards afterward, they are merely used as "mixers."

Getting down to business

Hand out the syllabus and guidelines and have the class read them (see Appendix I and II for examples).

A class session begins with a brief lecture to give students an idea of what they are about to learn through improv. A specific theme of exploration is isolated for each meeting. The first session lecture is something of an overview. The following, of course, are just notes, not a recipe.

ORIENTATION LECTURE NOTES

Acting is a way of exploring oneself. It is the total development of a human being into the most he can be and in as many directions as he can possibly take. Most people are capable of enormous amounts of creativity and humor. What stands in the way of the expression of these attributes is *fear* of making fools of ourselves. In her *Book of Answers,* author Barbara Berliner said that a poll of 3,000 Americans showed that fear of speaking in front of a group leads all other fears. Next are fear of heights, insects, financial problems and deep water. Acting allows you the freedom to let go, to be in the moment, and to be spontaneous. Gradually, you may no longer have the fear of losing or of failure.

In order to trigger creativity and humor, we are going to use a two-step process.

First, we will remove the *fear* by creating a safe environment that is warm, friendly, playful and nonjudgmental, where students can let down those safeguards against looking foolish and discard mental blocks.

Second, we will go through a series of exercises that help spark creativity and start the humor flowing. If we can get the students comfortable and relaxed and give them intriguing things to do, out should come performances that are awe-inspiring.

In developing self-awareness through drama, it is helpful to have a place where students can explore and fall on their faces. This prevents them from switching to automatic pilot and becoming congealed into their final selves.

INDIVIDUAL SELF-INTRODUCTIONS

After the opening lecture in the first session, individuals introduce themselves to the rest of the class. No pressure is put on students to perform. If a member chooses to pass during the introductions — or, for that matter, in any of the exercises — he may do so until he feels comfortable.

It helps to outline how to do it:

1. Interact with previous speaker, remembering his name with a comment. This is because for some time,

you will be dependent on each other as a group.

2. *Breathe.*

3. Make eye contact with the audience and state your name.

4. Give *one word* to describe yourself.

5. Tell your occupation.

6. Give any theatrical background you may have.

7. State why you are taking this class and what you hope to gain.

In order to ease the tension of the introductions — the first time on stage, and *alone* — add a "Nairobi Trio" à la Ernie Kovacs to the action. Three students sit in chairs on the stage, wearing grotesque rubber half-masks and black derbies. One has a dead cigar in his mouth. Each is given an instrument — a bongo drum, a set of rhythm sticks and a tambourine. As students enter and exit before and after their introductions, the terrible trio proceeds to "play." The member with the rhythm sticks, while still keeping time, sometimes turns and hits another member lightly on the head. All reactions among the three are slow. During the actual introductions they remain frozen so as not to distract. At the end of the students' introductions, one member of the trio at a time takes off his mask and derby, puts down his instrument, introduces himself and exits the stage. The last "musician" is left alone to present the final introduction without accompaniment. A big hand is given to the good-natured performers of this improvisational trio. This sets the tone for the zaniness of the class.

Now for the improvs themselves:

EXERCISES

Pocket Profile

To ensure random pairing off for this improv, match up people from different parts of the room, making certain that friends sitting with each other are not grouped. In twos, they should have five minutes or so to exchange two articles from their pockets or purses. They will then be called on-stage to tell the audience about each other, a brief profile, based on the two articles — keys, credit cards, theatre stubs or whatever.

Examples:

Power objects show independence (i.e., Jaguar keys).

Items such as credit cards could indicate sexual revolution, consumption, no unfulfilled desires, instant gratification and belonging.

Drivers' licenses could mean authority, permission to drive, also, conforming.

Movie ticket stubs could mean distraction or a dream machine.

(Have fun with this. Don't go too deep or be too analytical. It is *not* psychodrama.)

Or, the director can use the following improv:

Pantomime Communication

What we *think* we are communicating may not be true. Two actors go on-stage. One pantomimes a message to the other, who then relates what he thinks has been communicated. Now, reverse roles.

ASSESSMENT

Ask the class: What did you learn today? Then hold an open discussion.

PREVIEW OF NEXT CHAPTER

Finally, there should be a short preview of the next class meeting. Its **theme of exploration** will be **improvisation.**

Assignment (for the next meeting)

A one-minute solo presentation in which each actor

8

will sell something — himself, an idea or a product. (Good salesmanship requires enthusiasm, energy, conviction, knowledge of subject and a good "close.")

Or, the instructor can assign each member of the class to make a one-minute presentation concerning a totem or emblem that has symbolized his life. These should be shown, if possible.

Or, assign one-minute "Academy Award" speeches. Each actor is to present what he would say on that momentous occasion.

Or, each student displays and tells in one minute about an object from his closet.

Or, make no assignment, but start the next class with "Add a Story." Three actors on-stage. One actor begins a story, instructor rings bell, second actor picks up story and after another bell third actor brings it to a close.

Chapter 2
IMPROVISATION

Assignment for this session: One minute solo salesmanship presentations.

Or, one-minute presentations of totems.

Or, one-minute Academy Award speeches.

Or, one-minute "Object From My Closet" show and tell.

Or, add a story.

LECTURE NOTES

Improvisation is one of the most valuable tools an actor can possess. Knowing how to improvise supplies an actor with the ability to react with imagination to any situation and to develop instant dramatic or humorous sets of circumstances. Improv teaches actors to play off each other and become self-reliant as well as confident. Improv is a combined effort — not the result of one actor dominating the scene. *It is collaboration* — a communion in planning. The trick is not to block action initiated by another actor onstage. Go with the flow. For instance, if an actor states that a second actor has bloodstains on his clothing, instead of saying, "No, I don't," the second actor picks up the idea and counters with "It's grape juice" or "A tomato hit me."

Through improvisation, the actor experiences fresh images, learns the value of flexibility, concentration, observation, communication and teamwork.

In *evaluating* improv, it is not whether it was bad or good, but what works and doesn't work. Did it fulfill the assigned exercise?

The structure of improv is made up of WHO, WHAT, WHERE and HOW.

WHO: (relationships).

11

WHAT: (focus — activity, involvement, conflict, problem).

WHERE: (the setting).

HOW: (the process — the way the scene is played).

The actors: In improv, the actors need to avoid the HOW. How the exercise will develop evolves on the stage, keeping spontaneity and moment of discovery. (The conflict is solved during the action, not in preparation.) The actors are to concentrate only on the WHO, WHAT and WHERE.

The audience: During the improv, the class members will be evaluating the WHO, WHAT, WHERE *and* the HOW.

In advanced classes, two other Ws may be added: WHEN and WHY.

Sample improv

After the lecture, call two actors to the stage and set up a sample improv. This begins with a small, everyday occurrence. One element is added at a time.

Example:

WHERE: A living room and an office.

WHO: A mother and her rocket-scientist son.

WHAT (conflict): Accusative mother phoning the son.

HOW: They sit back to back, each with a telephone.

Actors develop the improv with no previous planning. Perhaps the mother reduces the guilt-ridden son to a blithering idiot child.

Before each improv, shuffle cards bearing the students' names, drawing randomly to form groups — preferably two or three at a time. This "student shuffle" prevents the same people from working together too frequently.

Each group waits its turn in the "wings." If there is no

off-stage space or screen, the students turn their backs until ready to enter. After setting their scenery and props, they signal the beginning of the action with a word or two. In our group they called out "S.O.S." (Students on Stage), thus telling the audience that the improv was beginning.

One of the goals is to be a *minimal* artist. Actors choose the barest thread of an improv, onto which can hang behavioral and character action. Little negotiations, not necessarily accomplishing things — as in life. Minimalism is the idea of putting a magnifying glass on small moments and issues, making something out of next to nothing. This concept is encouraged throughout the classes.

IMPROV EXERCISES

First Group Improv

Using the minimalist approach, two actors portray characters with decidedly different personalities. Say he is persistent, she is reluctant; or she is fretful, he is oblivious, etc. But even with these differing personalities, they have the continuing ability to survive trivial conflicts.

Student shuffle.

Each pair of actors is given a WHO, WHAT and WHERE minimalist situation by the instructor.

For example:

WHO: Married couple.

WHERE: Inside automobile.

WHAT (conflict): They are lost, but he won't ask directions.

Or:

WHO: Married couple.

WHERE: Living room.

WHAT: She wants him to rearrange furniture.

Or:

WHO: Two friends.

WHERE: At a bar.

WHAT: Supposedly talking to each other, but relating own subject matter. (i.e., He talking baseball, and she's talking therapy.)

Or:

WHO: Man and woman.

WHERE: Table at a coffee shop.

WHAT: Blind date.

Etcetera.

The Waiting Line

WHERE: Standing in a line. (For example at a bank, market, movie, restaurant, telephone booth, etc., as suggested by instructor.)

WHAT (conflict): Waiting, utilizing minimalist situations such as: Person with hiccups, person late and agitated, or person who has gum on his shoe.

WHO: This is left up to the students.

Student shuffle.

ASSESSMENT

What did you learn today?

PREVIEW OF NEXT CHAPTER

Theme of exploration

Development of an ongoing character for the semester. Characters may be a blank canvas on which to practice the weekly exercises. The actor can hide behind a character, disappear into the role. Perhaps he will pretend to be six feet tall, bearded, with a hearing aid and sore feet.

Assignment

A one-minute description by each student of his ongoing character. The character can be alive, dead, real or fictional. Handouts to help create the character include the outline of the character's history, examples of characters created from the inside and characters created from the outside (see Appendices III, IV and V).

Chapter 3
TECHNIQUES OF CHARACTER DEVELOPMENT

LECTURE NOTES

The joy of acting is getting to play characters who are not you, exploring the dark, hidden sides of yourself. There are two main tools for character development — observation and emotional memory. Laurence Olivier had nothing but impatience with the Method acting technique of building a character out of the actor's own experience. Instead, he used observation, always constructing his character from details he observed in real life or developed from the character's experience in place of his own.

The first tool to characterization is *observation*. Helen Hayes said, "Acting talent is an alert awareness of other people." From a continual process of observing, true characterizations are born. Attempt to piece together gestures and mannerisms from different people to help form your character. These can come from friends, neighbors, relatives, strangers and other actors.

Perhaps the most important character trait is the *walk*. An accomplished actor can tell an audience who he is with just his walk. Helen Hayes, whose 1935 portrayal of Victoria Regina was described as "one of the finest historical performances in modern theatre," explained, "I couldn't get Victoria until I got her walk. She bounced — but with great authority."

Anthony Hopkins as Dr. Hannibal Lecter in *Silence of the Lambs* said, "I had immediate connection with the character. I knew his walk, I knew what he looked like, and I knew his voice."

The second tool in creating a character is *emotional memory*. In order to breathe life into a role, the actor needs emotional recall. If you are chosen to play a part that requires a specific emotion, where is the feeling of that emotion going to come from? Possibly from an event in your life when you experienced a similar sensation and can repeat expressions and gestures from that time. With observation and emotional memory, we begin to develop ongoing characters.

In *observation*, there are four levels of characterization: physical, social, psychological and moral. We are now going to portray age. As you observe people, are age qualities always physical? No. Age differences are part of an attitude toward life. An observed cliché of old age is white hair and stumbling along with a cane. It is possible to show age and feelings with feet, elbows, hands and voice. *Show, not tell!*

Assignment for this week

A solo one-minute description of your ongoing character. Create a whole psyche that may never be seen or brought out, but makes the character three-dimensional. For instance, Stan Laurel never cried because he was hurt or scared. He only cried when he was confused and did not know what to do. Give your ongoing character a history — add flesh and bone. (If the student has trouble describing his character, the instructor can ask questions about speech pattern, body movement, props, hobbies, etc.)

IMPROV EXERCISES

How Old Am I? (An observation improv)

WHERE: Bus stop.

WHAT (conflict): Waiting. Include minimalist actions such as humming, tapping a foot, dropping things, etc.

WHO: This is left up to the students. Convey age.

Student shuffle. (Perhaps four or five in a team.)

18

Actors remain on-stage after the improv for:

Audience evaluation — How old were they? Did they *show*, not *tell*?

How Do I Feel? *(An emotional memory improv)*

WHERE: Same bus stop.

WHO: Same characters.

WHAT (conflict): Show a given emotion called for on a card drawn at random (anger, shyness, excitement, etc.). Keep the word with you. Do not divulge it until after audience evaluation.

ASSESSMENT

What did you learn today?

PREVIEW OF NEXT CHAPTER

Theme of exploration

Ensemble playing (working with others). This includes talking, *listening* and reacting. *Acting is reacting!* Let your *body* listen as well as your brain.

Assignment

In one minute and in the manner of your ongoing character, tell a single important fact about that character to another actor. He, in turn, will relate an important fact about his character to you. *Listen, react!*

Chapter 4
ENSEMBLE

The three most important words in ensemble acting are *trust, support* and *cooperation*. Without these basic qualities, successful improv work with others cannot be accomplished. Ensemble work means that each performer relates to and enriches the others. Shakespeare called actors "players," which suggests having fun. Ensemble playing is sharing the stage picture with other players. Listening and reacting. Acting *is* reacting. Let your *body* listen and react as well as your *brain*. How does the audience know what the characters are to each other? By the way they *interact*. This involves discipline and intuition. Until the actors are truly listening and reacting with each other, the transactions between characters are not vivid and the scene lacks interest. Individual playing only reaches full effectiveness in interaction with other performers.

Ensemble playing involves one character's attempt to force his will on another. This supplies the essential element of conflict. The transfer of energy from one character to another through the action-reaction chain allows the scene to develop.

Simple rules for ensemble playing:

— Do not move when the other actor is talking. Move on your own lines.

— Keeping in character, listen, react and respond.

Ensemble utilizes eye contact, personal space, open and closed positions (facing toward or away, arms folded over chest, etc.) and touching. Actors do not distract or upstage. Actors employ stage balance, "dressing the stage" and countering to balance. (In other words, actors position themselves to enhance the scene.)

21

DEMONSTRATION OF STAGE BALANCE

Five (an uneven or unbalanced number) actors on-stage wearing eye masks of different colors supplied by instructor. Actors remain silent, but group and regroup as instructor calls out their mask colors. ("Orange, move to purple . . .," etc.) The audience is observing grouping and regrouping on-stage and the effect it creates. Now, instructor tosses in a soft object such as a balloon or a rag doll. Continuing to remain silent, the masked actors group and regroup once again, reacting to this new element, which becomes an object of conflict.

Or, the leader may call out conflict situations for the actors to play against, such as fire, flood, earthquake, UFO, heat wave or flying insects.

DEMONSTRATION OF PHYSICAL ENSEMBLE

The instructor removes the conflict and adds a common bond to the same five masked actors. Still with no dialog, they are held together by a chain, a rope, a long stick, a thread, a circle of elastic or even an invisible connector. The actors are to project ensemble playing while bound together.

Or, the leader may verbally call out a common bond such as fear, excitement, hysteria, caution, sadness, boredom, embarrassment, disappointment, confusion, guilt or secretiveness.

The remainder of the class goes through the same routines in uneven groups.

Assignment

In the manner of their ongoing characters, two actors meet. Each relates one brief, important fact about himself. Concentrate on listening, reacting and eye contact. Begin off-stage with *silent tension*. Tensing and relaxing the body from head to toe reduces brain activity, which helps actors concentrate on effective ensemble work and adds suspense and energy. *Get out of your head.*

IMPROV EXERCISES

Telephone Time

Three actors sit in chairs facing the audience. There is a telephone in front of each. At the instructor's bell, all pick up receivers and begin talking softly. One actor raises his voice and projects a conversation without looking at the others. A second actor picks one word from that conversation to begin talking on his own telephone and projects over the first actor's voice. The third picks a word from the second and uses it in yet another conversation. At no time do the three actors relate to each other. The two "faded out" actors do not "freeze," but continue to talk softly and pantomime as they go out of focus.

For example, the first actor could be calling his travel agent and uses the word "Baja." The second actor picks up the phone and says "Baja, humbug! You have stood me up for the last time." The third actor may say, "The last time? The last time I saw you, you were a blonde."

And on and on . . .

Student shuffle. *Or:*

Give and Take

WHERE: A restaurant.

WHAT: Ensemble playing.

WHO: This is left up to the students.

There are two chairs and a table on each side of the stage to create the restaurant scene. Two pairs of actors sit at the tables. Neither pair relates to the actors at the other table. Each pair, having been given a topic by the instructor or the audience, stages an independent scene. At a signal from the instructor, both sets of actors start dialogs. At a second signal, Team A continues dialog while Team B fades from focus, but continues soft conversation, *does not freeze*. Focus shifts back and forth on signal.

After various combinations of class members have gone through this exercise, they can return to the stage and ensemble play *without* signals from the instructor.

ASSESSMENT

What did you learn today?

PREVIEW OF NEXT CHAPTER

Theme of exploration

Physicalization. Showing an emotion physically. Actors need to act with the whole body as an expressive instrument involving movement and gestures. This is not pantomime. If changing inner action is shown only through facial mannerisms, actors are performing, not creating. What does happiness or sadness do to an actor physically?

Assignment

A one-minute scene in the manner of ongoing characters, physicalizing an inner emotion through a body change. Exaggerate for this exercise. Body language should enhance and match the dialog. For instance, a person using angry words would display tense body movements. On the other hand, a character might hide his feelings with an outward display of bravado.

Chapter 5
PHYSICALIZATION

One of the first principles of acting is *physicalize!* To physicalize is to act with the *whole* body as an expressive instrument. Think of it as *E-motion.* If changing *inner* action is shown only through facial mannerisms, actors are performing and not creating. Physicalization is *not* pantomime. It is showing a physical expression of an attitude during dialog. Not telling, showing. Telling comes from the head, showing comes from intuition. In communicating to an audience, the role played by *words* does not exceed 35 percent! The balance of communication relies on nonverbal cues through movement and gestures. An actor can express less through words than with a pause, a swallow or tensed shoulders. The physical traits of body and voice are the means the actor has to create a character. Inner emotion can be physicalized through muscular awareness, including facial expression, posture, breathing, bodily positions and gestures.

But can an actor ever be too physical so that he distracts from the scene? The answer is yes. A suggestion of physicalization is needed, not frenetic movement with no purpose behind it. For instance, a suggestion of hiccups or stuttering or a limp.

Suppose the actor is portraying age. What happens physically in the aging process? The clichés of old age include the querulous voice, stiff joints, a bent back, canes, unsteady walk and fading vision and hearing. But what if the character has been very active? He rode horses, managed a business or skydived. How would that character look and act physically even though he is a senior citizen?

Movement is the one speech that does not lie. If an

actor is physically expressive, the audience does not perceive any acting occurring.

Assignment

Show an emotion physically. A one-minute scene *in your ongoing character*, physicalizing an inner emotion through a body change. Each actor will wear an eye mask supplied by instructor in order that the audience may concentrate on the body movements instead of facial expressions and so that the actor does not rely on facial expressions.

IMPROV EXERCISES

The Body Shows

Two actors walk at random on-stage. Instructor commands, "Freeze!" Audience is asked to state what each actor is saying with his body. Actors then begin a minimalist improv with appropriate dialog and action. Thus, the scene develops from the physical positions.

Student shuffle.

WHERE Improv

One member of a team steps downstage and creates a reality by starting a physical action indicating a WHERE. The remaining actors begin demonstrating movements that put them in the same WHERE, creating a place that the audience can identify. No dialog.

Student shuffle.

Hold It!

WHAT (conflict): In groups of five, physicalize given attitudes. Each actor selects an attitude and holds it throughout a scene. The choices are listed on an on-stage sign. They are:

1. Belligerent chin and expanded chest.
2. Petulant mouth and hunched shoulders.
3. Wide-eyed and firm, aggressive step.

28

4. Frowning and pigeon-toed.

5. Smiling and stiff-necked.

WHO: This is left up to the students.

WHERE: This is left up to the students.

Groups are selected by the student shuffle.

Preparation time: Five minutes for each team member to choose attitudes, decide on a minimalist topic and the WHO and the WHERE. For instance: what movie to see; what restaurant to go to.

Audience Evaluation

Did the actors physicalize and hold their attitudes?

Machine

Each group of five actors, wearing eye masks, combines to form a machine. The first actor enters and begins a movement to which he adds a sound. The second actor enters, hooks up with the first actor, begins a different movement and a new sound. The third, fourth and fifth follow suit until all five seem to be parts of a working machine. The instructor calls out, "faster" to speed up the action and "slower" to wind it down. Then, one by one, in reverse order, they break off and exit, leaving the first actor alone with his movement and sound.

Sculpture

Five actors, again in eye masks, each select a card upon which is written an emotion. On-stage, hiding the cards from the audience, they become a sculpture at the instructor's signal, each portraying the chosen emotion. The audience evaluates them, after which the actors display the cards to show whether their portrayals were accurate. The emotions are:

1. Anger

2. Happiness

3. Despair

4. Fear

5. Embarrassment

Object Moves Actors

Five actors, again in eye masks, are directed by the instructor to physicalize involvement with a large inanimate object. These objects can include:

1. Revolving door
2. Hot-air balloon
3. Elevator
4. Merry-go-round
5. Roller coaster
6. Sailboat
7. Ferris wheel

Build a Character

This one is performed in groups of three, selected by the student shuffle. On-stage, the first actor throws out the first name of an imaginary character. The second actor supplies a middle name. The third actor adds a surname.

The first actor begins to describe the character, perhaps stating he is a man with one arm. The second actor might say, "He is stooped and has a beard down to his knees." The third actor might add, "He sings to himself and is pigeon-toed."

The first actor begins to move around the stage, physicalizing the invented character. The second actor joins him with his interpretation. The third offers his own physicalization and all three exit as the imaginary character.

ASSESSMENT

What did you learn today?

PREVIEW OF NEXT CHAPTER

Theme of exploration

Sustaining.

Assignment

Sustain a one-minute scene in your ongoing character that holds the audience's attention and interest.

Chapter 6
SUSTAINING

Sustaining in the theatre means to hold the audience's curiosity — to prolong a scene or action while keeping the audience's interest. Once interest ceases, it is difficult, often impossible, to renew the audience's attention. How does the actor sustain his mood through the entire performance? There is a technique to sustaining. The trick is to make it feel that what is happening on-stage is happening for the first time, every time. This, of course, is the key to improvisation. The improv is happening for the first time — not rehearsed. Through high energy, body language (physicalization), projection, emotion and character development, actors sustain the action and the audience's involvement.

The sustaining of a pause is one of the most effective elements in performance art. Jack Benny, perhaps the ultimate minimalist in American comedy, was the master of pauses. His timing was perfection. The classic illustration was the radio sketch in which a stick-up man confronted the notorious pennypincher and demanded, "Your money or your life." As audience laughter built steadily, a long, long pause threatened to become an endless wait before Benny delivered the famous punch line: "I'm thinking! I'm thinking!"

Assignment

Sustain a one-minute scene in your ongoing character that holds the audience's attention, curiosity and interest.

IMPROV EXERCISES

In the Mood

WHAT (conflict): Group sustains a given mood in a minimalist improv.

WHO: Suggested by instructor or audience.

WHERE: Suggested by instructor or audience.

A card drawn at random states the mood. The card is not shown to the audience until after the improv. Example of moods:

Fear	Premonition
Excitement	Serenity
Gloom	Agitation
Happiness	

Student shuffle.

Examples of minimalist topics: Where to go on vacation or what to buy for a wedding present.

Telephone Talk

WHAT: Two actors on two telephones sit back to back. Sustain conversation, with meaningful pauses, about a given topic selected from a card drawn at random.

WHO: Suggested by instructor or audience.

WHERE: Suggested by instructor or audience.

Possible minimalist topics:

Relatives

Work

Movies

Vacation

Student shuffle.

The Dining Room

WHERE: A dining room.

WHO: Supplied by instructor or audience.

WHAT (conflict): Supplied by instructor or audience.

Possible activities:

Party	Card game
Holiday dinner	Seance

Reading of a will   Lingerie sales pitch

Student shuffle.

Confined

WHAT (conflict): A situation involving confinement.

WHO: Supplied by instructor or audience.

WHERE: Supplied by instructor or audience.

Possible situations:

> Robbers hiding in a closet or bank vault
>
> Trapped in a pit or a cave-in
>
> Trapped by guard dogs
>
> Lost in an underground garage
>
> Self-confined
>
> Imprisoned
>
> Lighthouse keeper
>
> Stalled elevator
>
> On an island
>
> In a haunted house

Student shuffle.

ASSESSMENT

What did you learn today?

PREVIEW OF NEXT CHAPTER

Theme of exploration

Vocal technique, clear and effective speech, projection, articulation and enunciation (distinct pronouncing of words).

Assignment

A one-minute speech in your ongoing character titled "What the World Needs Now."

Chapter 7
VOCAL TECHNIQUE

Vocal technique includes sharing your voice with an audience through projection, articulation, enunciation and pauses. To improve projection by relaxing the throat, the pyramid exercise is useful. This consists of positioning an actor so he is facing the director and pressing the latter's palms forcefully with his own while turning his head and speaking to the audience. In this position, his vocalization comes from his diaphragm instead of his throat. This can be practiced by the actor at home or before stage entrance by simply leaning forward and pushing the hands against a wall or door jamb while projecting his voice.

Enunciation is distinct pronunciation. It is fine for a character to sputter if this is called for, but the actor must not swallow syllables or mumble (except for Marlon Brando).

Articulation is clear and effective speech. Articulation expresses much about the intellectual aspects of the character. For example, Dustin Hoffman in the film *Midnight Cowboy* and Sylvester Stallone in the movie *Rocky*.

Utilize pauses to allow impact to sink in. Wait. Hold back. Pauses are a valuable and creative tool. They can indicate that the character is trying to remember something or attempting to reach a decision. Pauses can sustain a scene, add to the characterization and are often more effective than dialog. In good silent moments, all the talking can take place in the audience's heads.

Before each presentation, check for tension in the throat. The four tools of good diction are lips, tongue, teeth and a relaxed throat. A tape recorder at home is the best instrument to learn about your own voice, to hear how you sound and deliver language.

Strive for expressiveness. Inflection is the emphasis within a word. Work for individuality in your speech, not necessarily attractiveness. Three unattractive laughs can be practiced with the students. A laugh emanating from the back of the throat, a laugh through an overbite and a laugh with lips closed.

Use subtlety, not overacting as in melodrama. Make your speech interesting as opposed to monotonous unless the character calls for the latter — for example, the lack of emotion displayed by Peter Sellers in the film *Being There* and Dustin Hoffman in the movie *Rainman*.

Be aware of pitch, tempo and emphasis (or punch).

Before entrance, practice deep breathing from the diaphragm, bend over, shake your body out, try some head rotations, shoulder shrugs, jaw drop and rubber band lips.

Assignment

A one-minute speech in your ongoing character titled "What the World Needs Now." Remain on-stage. Instructor directs:

1. Move upstage and perform a stage whisper, then a shout with relaxed throat.

2. Use the expression "Don't go" with an inflection registering whatever feeling is called out by the director, such as:

   Beg, alarm, warn, surprise, seduce, sly, timid, mysterious, sad, grateful, angry, fearful, disappointed, frustrated, teasing, excited, forgiving, threatening, impetuous, comical, scornful, menacing or incredulous.

3. Call out "Yeah, yeah, yeah" in any manner to exit.

IMPROV EXERCISES

WHAT (conflict): Three unrelated words, on cards chosen at random, are woven into an improv sketch and

38

must be clearly heard by the audience. The cards, which are displayed for the audience, may carry such combinations as:

Eraser, tractor, pantyhose.

Hanger, shadow, toothbrush.

Jello, newspaper, ambulance.

WHO: Supplied by instructor or audience.

WHERE: Supplied by instructor or audience.

Student shuffle.

Vocalization

The class is divided into three groups.
1. Calling out (such as from a cave, a mountaintop or a forest).
2. Stage whisper (from a jail, for instance, a bank vault, a church or a library).
3. Argument (over money, perhaps, in-laws, or a vacation trip).

ASSESSMENT

What did you learn today?

PREVIEW OF NEXT CHAPTER

Theme of exploration

Pantomime.

Assignment

One-minute pantomime in your ongoing character. No dialog. No human sounds; noises OK. No props. Costume pieces OK. Concentrate on muscular awareness — physicalization. Involve both face and the whole body. Main elements of pantomime: Simplicity, clarity — no fuzziness. Definite beginnings and endings of movements. The movements should be so clear that they are not confused with any others. Slow down and exaggerate.

Chapter 8
PANTOMIME

Pantomime. The first level of characterization is physical — for instance, the character's walk. Emotion, such as anger, boredom or tenderness, can be conveyed through silence and constantly finds expression in bodily position. Therefore, pantomime is of primary importance to actors. It is language without words. It is acting in which all physical images are stylized. Gestures are used sparingly, but are intensified. The secret to successful pantomime is economy — of movement, mannerisms, handling of invisible objects and gestures. All gestures are enlarged, bigger than life and exaggerated. But it is very important to avoid an overflow of gestures.

The two main elements of pantomime are simplicity and clarity — no fuzziness. The actor needs definite beginnings and endings to all movements. In other words, each movement should be completed before another is begun.

Movements need to honestly interpret sizes and shapes of objects. The audience is allowed to see the actor's exaggerated gesture of a hand opening and closing around an object so that the object's size and shape are clearly projected. The actor must not violate boundaries of imaginary objects already established. Example: Do not walk through an established wall or table. A requirement of the *professional* mime is the ability to remember the height of a table or the placement of a wall. This ability is called the "clic." The nonprofessional can merely hope to approximate this goal.

The only sounds made in pantomime are those of objects. No human sounds allowed. For example: the swish of bullets, squeaking of doors and popping of corks supplied by an off-stage sound person are accepted conventions, but the sounds of people are not. When actors laugh, sneeze or cry, it is done silently and communicated only through movement.

The instructor may find it helpful to practice with the students silent laughs, sneezes, cries, sighs and handclaps.

Besides simplicity, pacing and timing of pantomime are important. Also vital is the manner of movement, posture and gestures. Are they consistent with the needs of the character? For example, a character who is ill would not have a spry walk — unless trying to mask his problem.

The state the actor should be in when performing — especially in pantomime — is high energy combined with physical relaxation. Thus, the practice of "silent tension," tightening each body part and then relaxing, before entrance is valuable. Stage energy is higher than life energy, but when the actor is relaxed, with no muscular tension, pantomime technique should not be apparent.

Assignment

A one-minute pantomime in your ongoing character. (The actor may state at the outset whom he is portraying.) No dialog. No human sounds. Noises OK. No props. Costume pieces OK. Concentrate on muscular awareness (physicalization) of face and body. Remain on-stage after presentation. The instructor calls out an inanimate object, which the actor then portrays, such as:

Clock	Tree
Telephone	Television set
Record player	Garbage can
Refrigerator	Typewriter
Electric fan	Light bulb
Trombone	Piano
Umbrella	Hammer
Vacuum cleaner	Clothes dryer

Accordian   Pencil

Scissors   Coffee pot

IMPROV EXERCISES

Where Are We?

WHAT (conflict): To show where the actors are through pantomime.

WHERE: Suggested by instructor or audience.

WHO: Suggested by instructor or audience.

The groups work together to indicate WHERE by seeing, listening, relationships, activity and handling of invisible objects.

Student shuffle.

Silent Film

WHERE: Stage of a silent film company.

WHAT (conflict): A "director" chosen by instructor uses pantomime to explain desired action to small group of actors.

WHO: Indicated with hats or other costume pieces (supplied by instructor) selected by "director," who then pantomimes filming the developing improv.

Student shuffle.

Make Sense of It

The students are divided into three groups.

First group pantomimes seeing something (such as a sport).

Second group pantomimes listening to something.

Third group pantomimes tasting something.

ASSESSMENT

What did you learn today?

PREVIEW OF NEXT CHAPTER

Theme of exploration

Props.

Assignment

A one-minute scene in your ongoing character handling a prop or props.

Chapter 9
PROPS

Awareness of props is a starting point for developing scenes. This awareness includes use of intuition and imagination. Improvs can even be shaped from the props themselves. How the character handles the prop indicates to the audience the ease of incorporation into the role. Examples: Charlie Chaplin's cane and George Burns's cigar. It is a good idea to personalize the prop from the point of view of the character. In other words, try not to use it conventionally. For instance, Laurel and Hardy's costume derbies became their distinctive props.

A well-chosen prop or props may say a lot about the character. Material culture and consumer products can be used, and abused, for self-definition (such as a briefcase), character judgments (cigarettes), or as currency in interpersonal relationships (furs, jewelry, etc.). While props do not provide the complete definition for a character, they give more detail and specificity. In other words, they help set time and place.

Props can sometimes save or enrich scenes by becoming attention-getting or conversational aids. The inventive craft that Peter Falk has brought to *Columbo* on television includes his choice of props. He believes that if the actor is left with only words, he is in trouble. Falk's answer is to always look for props that will help motivate behavior. This way the charater is not solely dependent on language. Thus, his very small notebook, his *lack* of a pen or pencil and his cigar help illuminate his persona.

Cigars, cigarettes and pipes are gradually disappearing as props. The use of cigarettes now is assigned mostly to villains, who are almost obligated to light up. Just the manner of striking a match can indicate much about a character. Many actors bring to their roles the various uses to which they put cigarettes in their own lives: to pause, to pose, to control, to share or to play for time in an awkward situation.

The way in which the actor personalizes props can make a performance memorable. The prop can be a key to the character. The jaunty manner in which Chaplin twirled his cane displayed his cheerfulness and refusal to be defeated by circumstances. He treated inanimate objects as though they were conscious. Jack Benny's violin served to heighten his pretensions. And Mae West's boa helped to exaggerate her comedic sexiness.

Also, a prop can enhance a scene's action. In an episode of the Jerry Seinfeld television show, which took place in an underground mall garage, a large, heavy box containing a television set and a plastic bag filled with live fish became the focal point of the entire half-hour show. Would the box safely reach its destination? Would the fish still be alive by the time the principals found their car?

An unusual service a prop may perform: It might tell you how a play or an improv is going. In the one-man Broadway show, *Tru*, Robert Morse won a Tony for his portrayal of Truman Capote. A framed portrait of Capote as a young man was a vital prop in the performance. Finally, in one scene, the actor snatched up the picture and angrily put his fist through it. At each showing, the audience gasped. The audience knew the painting was just a prop, but what the gasp said was that the audience believed in what went before. Thus, the prop can sometimes make an excellent barometer.

A word of caution: A wise actor always double-checks his own props rather than leave it entirely to a prop person, if one exists. What happens when props are missing or don't work? In one scene of a play, a letter opener was gone. The actor turned and in place of stabbing his startled opponent, proceeded to kick him, meanwhile saying, "It's good my shoe has a poisoned tip!" Whereupon, the quick-witted co-actor fell to the floor.

If there is an accident with a prop on-stage, incorporate it into the scene. For instance, in a Broadway production of *Lucifer's Child*, Julie Harris, as writer Isak Dinesen, had to cope with a large oil painting that tumbled to the floor in mid-soliloquy. The actress never missed a beat as she ad-libbed to cover the accident, resumed her speech, picked up the fallen prop and then, chattering all the while, waited for exactly the right pause that would allow her to replace the canvas without further blemishing the mood of the play.

Props can be vitally important. Sometimes a prop can even become a character. For instance: the paintings in the movies *Picture of Dorian Gray* and *Laura*; the diary in the motion picture about Anne Frank, the statuette in *The Maltese Falcon*, and the model house in the play *Tiny Alice*.

A memorable prop was used in an *Alfred Hitchcock Presents* TV episode entitled "Lamb to the Slaughter." Barbara Bel Geddes' character beat her husband to death with a frozen leg of lamb, then cooked and served it to police investigators as they puzzled over the whereabouts of the murder weapon.

It is important to always rehearse with props. They can do the most unexpected things. The author was once in final rehearsal as the daughter in Ruth Gordon's *Years Ago*, standing on a table, while her stage mother pretended to pin up the hem of her ankle-length dress with imaginary pins in place of the real thing. On opening night, she descended from the table and proceeded to walk across the stage. The real pins, not having been used in rehearsal, unexpectedly stuck her in the legs and ankles, causing her to exclaim — while staying in character — "Ow, the damn pins are sticking me!"

Assignment

One-minute scene in your ongoing character, handling a prop or props.

IMPROV EXERCISES

Paper Bag Theatre

Numerous brown paper shopping bags are each filled with six or seven miscellaneous props.

WHAT (conflict): Build an improv around all the props in your bag.

WHO: Left up to the students.

WHERE: Left up to the students.

Example of one bag's contents: A water bottle, a camera, a telephone, a flashlight and a broken tennis racquet.

Student shuffle.

Preparation time: Five minutes to examine props and decide WHO and WHERE.

Prop as a Character

Instructor assigns one prop to each group of actors.

WHAT (conflict): The prop becomes a character.

WHO: Left up to the students.

WHERE: Left up to the students.

This improv sets up emotions and different relationships directly involving actors through the prop. Example: Sell it, destroy it, build it, hide it or hide something in it.

Possible props: Foam rubber gravestone, a wallet, binoculars, a world globe, a sexy undergarment or a broken record.

Student shuffle.

Preparation time: Five minutes to devise WHO and WHERE, or an instant improv with no preparation.

Prop It Up

Five props are presented on-stage by instructor. Each group develops a scene around the same five props. Props could include a telephone, a clock, a typewriter, a letter, and an urn.

Student shuffle.

Preparation time: Five minutes to form WHAT, WHO and WHERE.

ASSESSMENT

What did you learn today?

PREVIEW OF NEXT CHAPTER

Theme of exploration

Imagination.

Assignment

A one-minute scene imagining your ongoing character in a supermarket. Whether that character is alive or dead, fictional or real, or whether he lived before supermarkets were invented, place him there.

Chapter 10
IMAGINATION

Imagination is the tool allowing the actor to believe and communicate what otherwise might be unbelievable. If the actor believes it, so will the audience. The purpose of cultivating an active imagination in the actor is to give a solid experience of living in a particular situation. The actor needs to revive that childlike approach to pretending. The ability to create a situation imaginatively and to play a role in it is a tremendous experience. Creative imagination involves a kaleidoscope of ideas. Most children are robbed of imagination in the early school years, being directed to think in absolute limited terms.

Creative imagination has the capacity to give actors space and freedom to explore. The imaginative actor takes the author's words, the director's interpretation, the costumer's clothes plus his own personality and makes the part the actor's invention.

In improv, however, the actor has no author's words, no director's interpretation — merely costume pieces and the actor's own personality. How does the improv actor create? Through body language (physicalization) and imagination. It is the actor's responsibility to make full use of imagination in formulating a characterization. All acting is make-believe, but actors can — with imagination and body language — create it to seem true.

Assignment

A one-minute scene in your ongoing character in a supermarket.

IMPROV EXERCISES

Build a WHERE

53

On the bare stage, one actor at a time adds an imaginary object to build a WHERE, such as: a pet store, a restaurant or a costume shop. After the first actor has placed an imaginary object in the setting that has been chosen, each ensuing actor must relate to a previously positioned imaginary object while adding his own. This continues until the WHERE is fully established for the audience.

Return to Go

WHAT (conflict): Begin a scene on-stage that involves an interruption. At scene's end, return to starting position.

WHO: Provided by instructor.

WHERE: Provided by instructor.

Examples: Imagine a:

Toy store — Toys come to life when proprietor leaves. Return to frozen position when he re-enters.

Elevator — People grouped facing forward. Elevator stops between floors. People react in various ways: Try to phone for help, begin to panic, etc. Elevator starts again. Passengers return to original positions.

School — Children sitting at desks. Begin to act up when teacher leaves the room. On teacher's return, they resume original positions.

Student shuffle.

Freeze Tag

Two actors begin improv using exaggerated body language until any member of the audience calls "Freeze!" Both actors on-stage stay frozen until new actor tags and replaces one of them. The replacement creates a new situation that begins in the same position. The replacement speaks first to begin new improv and indicates the WHO and the WHAT.

Unknown Presence

WHAT (conflict): Imagine reaction called for by instructor to an unknown presence.

WHO: Left up to students.

WHERE: Left up to students.

The students are divided into three groups. On-stage, one student is sitting in a chair, cloaked from shoulders to feet. A mask covers the entire face and a hat covers the head. This actor never moves. One-third of the group is to react to the unknown presence with *fear*. Another third is to react with *curiosity*. And the last third is to show *acceptance*.

ASSESSMENT

What did you learn today?

PREVIEW OF NEXT CHAPTER

Theme of exploration

Entrances and exits.

Assignment

Before and after. Sustain a one-minute scene in your ongoing character between entrance and exit that indicates where the character has been and where he is going. The actor needs to improvise in his mind what happens to the character before the moment of entrance and after exiting. The entrance and exit should be sharp and creative. Frame yourself, exaggerate entrance and exit for this exercise. Save any punch line until moment of exit. This makes the audience watch the actor all the way off.

Chapter 11
ENTRANCES AND EXITS

LECTURE NOTES

On entering, the actor needs to "take stage" as much as possible. In exiting, the creative actor leaves the audience with a final impression of the character. There should be a sharp focus on the actor, if only for a fleeting second, at the moment of entrance and exit. It is the sharpness in framing such details that adds clarity and often brilliance to the performance. It also helps set the tone for the character. The first moment a character enters the acting space, the audience makes judgments about who he is and why he has come. The playwright and director usually take care of this focusing, but many actors neglect this important point and entrances and exits become fuzzy.

In improv there is no playwright or director, so it is entirely up to the actor to automatically create sharp entrances and exits. "Enter on your upstage foot" is a dramatic rule to keep actors from "hiding" from the audience. In other words, by stepping forward on the foot farthest from members of the audience, the actor's body is partially turned toward them. But, there are more exciting and challenging ways to meet an audience. A few variations include:

Fly in	Scream in
Trip in	Dance in
Fall in	Talk in off-stage voice
Sing in	One part of body at a time
Laugh in	Enter from audience

An example of entering backwards was displayed by Pavlova, the famous dancer, who in portraying the dying swan, appeared with her back to the audience, slowly turning to reveal her blood-drenched breast.

57

Will Rogers would make his inimitable entrance by moseying on-stage carrying a rope, chewing gum, scratching his head and saying "Howdy." That's all, but audiences went wild.

In exiting, all of the above can be utilized, plus an over-the-head wave and the common seeming inability to find the curtain opening. One of the most famous exits was Chaplin's penguin walk into the distance twirling his cane. Another was Jimmy Durante's as he stepped from one pool of light to the other saying, "Goodnight Mrs. Calabash, wherever you are." A third was the clown, Emmett Kelly, who swept a spot of light into his dustpan as it got smaller and finally disappeared in a blackout.

Save your punchline for the moment of exit. This makes the audience watch you all the way off.

Assignment

Before and after. A sharp creative entrance and exit in your ongoing character. One-minute scene in between. Focus and frame yourself. Exaggerate entrance and exit for this exercise. Let the audience absorb you. Audience should know where the character has been and where he is going. For this, the actor needs to improvise in his mind what happens to his character before the moment of entrance and after exiting.

IMPROV EXERCISES

Enter and Exit

WHAT (conflict): Incorporate in the scene more than one entrance and exit for each character. Actors may couple up.

WHO: Supplied by instructor or audience.

WHERE: Supplied by instructor or audience.

Examples: Party, waiting room, library.

Student shuffle.

Two Actors Meet

WHAT (conflict): Exhibit emotion given on card chosen at random. Do not show card to audience. Examples: Sadness, anger, shyness, excitement.

WHO: Left up to students.

WHERE: Left up to students.

Two actors enter from opposite sides of the stage, displaying the given emotion, sustaining it through scene and exiting. Actors return to face audience, showing their cards for evaluation.

Student shuffle.

A Gathering

Divide the actors into three groups. Each group will build an improv around a busy WHERE supplied by instructor or audience. For example: a bar, a train station or a courtroom. Actors incorporate many exits and entrances, appearing and leaving either as a group, singly or in various numbers.

ASSESSMENT

What did you learn today?

PREVIEW OF NEXT CHAPTER

Theme of exploration

Gibberish. In place of sensible words, use crazy mixed-up words and sounds. Substitute letters, numbers, foreign words, or words out of context for more convincing acting without reliance on language. Feelings and body language (physicalization) predominate.

Assignment

A one-minute scene in your ongoing character, using gibberish. Props and costume pieces OK.

Chapter 12
GIBBERISH

LECTURE NOTES

Gibberish is spoken nonsense sounds. Often actors speak their lines while concentrating too much on the words and not enough on their purpose. Gibberish substitutes sounds, grunts, gutterals, growls, hisses and occasional real words like "pantyhose" for English. Sid Caesar is the king of gibberish. He can make nonsense sound like a foreign language. Caesar says he feels more communicative grunting and moving on-stage than speaking.

The purpose and value of gibberish is to illuminate emotion and body language. It is integration of sound with physical response which releases the actor from technical details and frees him to be spontaneous. Gibberish forces the actor to communicate with carriage, body movement, voice, tone and feeling. In place of sensible words, the actor uses crazy, mixed-up words, sounds, letters or numbers.

The point of the gibberish improv is to clearly get the actor's intention across. It is an exercise in the mastery of purposeful acting. Many directors will use gibberish in a rehearsal to relax the cast and loosen up the actors. Actors showing the most resistance to gibberish rely on words rather than experiencing. Often, actors who are tied to words can become fluent, flexible and colorful with gibberish. It forces the actor to show and not tell.

Pantomime will not achieve the same results as gibberish. Dialog and action are interdependent. Gibberish forces the visual performance to have equal weight with verbalization.

Assignment

A one-minute scene in your ongoing character using gibberish. Props and costume pieces OK.

IMPROV EXERCISES

Gibberish Dictionary

Three actors on-stage sitting apart in chairs facing the audience. The first actor stands and delivers a short "word" in gibberish. He sits. The second actor rises and explains the word to the audience. Then he makes up his own and sits. The third actor stands, gives a definition of this and then delivers yet another "word," which the first actor explains. This continues until the director calls a halt.

Student shuffle.

Gibberish Situations

WHAT (conflict): Two actors speak in gibberish.

WHERE: Given situation from card chosen at random. (i.e., Two people stuck in an elevator, a thief and his victim, or traveler and foreigner.)

WHO: Some shown on cards. Others created by actors.

The actors display their cards at the beginning of the improv to let the audience know what they supposedly are saying.

Student shuffle.

Fractured Fairy Tales

WHAT (conflict): Gibberish.

WHO: Fairy tale characters assigned by director.

WHERE: Depending on the fairy tale.

Examples: "Cinderella," "Little Red Riding Hood," "Jack and the Beanstalk."

Group Relations

WHAT (conflict): Debate or discussion in gibberish.

WHO: Seven given roles.

WHERE: Up to students.

Hanging around the neck of each actor is a card which

designates who he is. Example: philosopher, nurse, clown, chairman, debater, derailer and victim. All are debating or discussing in gibberish a topic supplied by instructor or audience.

Student shuffle.

ASSESSMENT

What did you learn today?

PREVIEW OF NEXT CHAPTER

Theme of exploration

Animals — their movements and sounds.

Assignment

Perform for one minute as a bird. Strut, flap your wings, chirp or sing. Speak bird. Character elements of a bird: carefree, unfixed in life, lands anywhere, sudden and unexpected continuous movements, animated, lively, lack of logic, irresponsible and aimless rhythm. Exceptions: large flightless birds, such as the emu or the ostrich, whose character element would be meticulous. Large birds have a stilted manner of picking up and placing legs and feet, long and erect neck, bold and brazen stare. Moves suddenly from static pose to fast speed. Slow raising and lowering of wings.

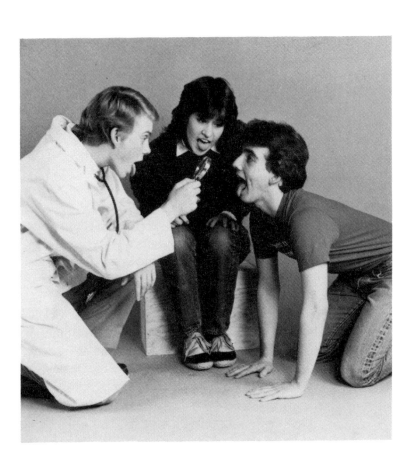

Chapter 13
ANIMALS

LECTURE NOTES

Feathers, fins and fur. The purpose of the animal exercise is to rid the actor of his social mask and free him from inhibitions. He learns how to use the body and voice differently. He moves away from feeling and concentrates on physical movement (physicalization). The animal exercise is used to teach actors to carry out unemotional tasks with muscular control. Animal images function as the beginning of character work. An animal can be the key to a characterization. The actor plays a human being with a chosen animal's different kind of walk, rhythm, behavior and attitude.

The primary emotions of the animal image can bring a totally new dimension to a role, giving the actor instant attributes on which to base his character — for instance: "He roars like a lion," "She's drunk as a skunk," "He is stubborn as a mule," or "He is sly as a fox."

In abstracting animal qualities to help create a role, it is helpful for the actor to see his surroundings from the animal's point of view. This takes pressure off of being one's self, and it can break the actor's basic patterns determined by habit. The animal exercise is good for actors who are out of touch with themselves.

Examples of animal characteristics used in human portrayals include Barbara Stanwyck's panther stride and Charles Laughton's squirrel-like movements while eating in bed during *Henry VIII*.

Assignment

Perform for a minute as a bird. Speak bird. Chirp, sing, honk, gabble, cluck, hoot or quack. Strut, flap your wings, physicalize a bird. Be a carefree bird or a meticulous bird.

In groups of four or five, the actors sit on-stage. One at a time, they rise to impersonate a bird, then resume their seats. When they are done, all rise and at the instructor's signal repeat their portrayals in chorus.

Student shuffle.

IMPROV EXERCISES

Noah's Ark

One actor plays Noah. He may be costumed with flowing robe, a staff, white beard and wig. From a list, he calls up the animals two by two. The actors enter and cross the stage in pairs, exhibiting their given animal characteristics as they exit to "enter the ark."

Lay It on the Other Actor

WHAT (conflict): One actor lays an animal quality on the other.

WHO: Left up to the students.

WHERE: Left up to the students.

Two actors enter the stage from opposite directions. One gets a jump on the other by quickly saying something like, "Oh, where did you get that hump on your back? You remind me of a camel." The second actor has to immediately take on the qualities of a humpback. He could retort, "Well, it's better than having feet like a duck!" The two exit, talking and exhibiting the animal characteristics.

Student shuffle.

Metamorphosis

WHAT (conflict): Transfer an animal's characteristics to a human being.

WHO: Suggested by instructor or audience.

WHERE: Suggested by instructor or audience.

The actors at first are to display an animal's characteristics in a short scene. At the instructor's signal, they change into human beings while retaining their chosen animals' qualities for a second short scene.

Student shuffle.

Animal Situations

WHAT (conflict): Exaggerate an animal's qualities throughout scene.

WHO: Character of choice with an animal's attributes.

WHERE: From situation cards chosen at random by each team (i.e.: a fashion show, a pickup bar, a gym).

Student shuffle.

The Jungle Book

WHERE: A jungle.

WHO: "The Jungle Book" characters.

WHAT: While a chosen narrator reads an abridged version of Rudyard Kipling's famous story, students assigned by the instructor act out the words in pantomime and with animal sounds.

ASSESSMENT

What did you learn today?

PREVIEW OF NEXT CHAPTER

Theme of exploration

Fantasy.

Assignment

Put your ongoing character in a French asylum during World War I.

Chapter 14
FANTASY

LECTURE NOTES

Fantasy incorporates the ability to suspend reality. Fantasies are made up from an inner life. They are not about rearranging thoughts, but rather depend on transformation and self-discovery. In real life there is often the need to escape into fantasy. Abandoning reality and thinking about things that are beyond our knowledge are similar to a vacation for the mind. Fantasies can also be used to solve problems. They may be tools to help us cope. For instance, if you are about to encounter a stressful situation, take time to envision the scene. Fantasize how you want to feel, how you want to behave and how you want to be treated. A fantasy rehearsal can prepare you with a supply of positive feelings.

The cult film *King of Hearts*, starring Alan Bates, supplies a rich background for a fanciful improv.

Assignment

WHO: In the manner of your ongoing character, you are inmates.

WHERE: An asylum in a French village.

WHEN: World War I.

WHAT: A stranger appears.

The story is an antiwar fantasy. A deserting soldier seeking to escape the horror of war enters the walled asylum. The inmates, confronted by someone from the outside (real) world, exhibit delusion, yet are tolerant of each others' fantasies. They remain to some degree inspired and free. There *is* madness, but not meanness. The improv concerns self-deception, human innocence and goodness. (The instructor chooses an actor to play the deserter.)

It helps to have the actors close their eyes and transform

69

themselves to a far-away time for a minute. Then they can take their places, in the manner of their ongoing characters, inside the asylum. This is the auditorium area in front of the stage. The soldier enters from the forest (back of the auditorium) and stands looking through an imaginary rusty iron gate. After a few moments the characters begin to notice the stranger and welcome him to their village, where he meets, perhaps, an Eleanor Roosevelt, Anne Frank or Charlie Chaplin, etc.

The inmates are so delighted with the stranger they decide to make him king. They take him up on-stage, crown him and drape his shoulders. (The cloth and crown are supplied by instructor.) The characters dance and sing around him. But the soldier, although enjoying himself, soon realizes he must return to his army post. He regretfully bids good-bye to the objecting villagers who stand at the gate waving after him.

He is returning to his "sane" world of war while they remain in their asylum.

IMPROV EXERCISES

Talking Heads

WHAT: Defending your life.

WHERE: Judgment city.

WHO: The dead (who may not know it).

This fantasy improv begins and ends with two grave-diggers (chosen by the instructor) in front of a screen of card tables turned on their sides. After a short improv in which the two gravediggers talk about anything or everything (à la *Waiting for Godot*) they exit. The first set of talking heads appear, their bodies hidden by the screen. Unable to use hands or body language, the actors must defend with just their words and expressions the way they have led their lives. Example: A politician, arguing with a constituent, may insist that he was honest.

The talking heads may include a *ménage à trois* — a man, his wife and his mistress dealing with the lies, deceptions, omissions and double-dealings of their lives.

Or perhaps three heads do not know each other. One could be an angel, one could be St. Peter, and one could be a chimney sweep.

Actors may add final traces of fleshly existence, such as hiccups, sneezes, stuttering, sniffles — but no hands. Maybe one's mouth feels dry, or one grinds his teeth. A head can utter prayers, sing songs or tell memories.

After the last improv of heads, the gravediggers reenter and close with their observations on life, or find a bone in the grave and exit quickly.

Student shuffle.

Mob Scene

WHAT: Relate to UFO.

WHERE: A field outside the community.

WHO: The actor's ongoing character.

ASSESSMENT

What did you learn today?

PREVIEW OF NEXT CHAPTER

Theme of exploration

Conflict.

Assignment

A one-minute scene in which your ongoing character bids good-bye.

Chapter 15
CONFLICT

Acting consists of overcoming obstacles. Conflict between characters provides interest and holds the audience's attention. Without conflict, there is no chance for creativity. Example: One actor states his wish for an activity and the second actor opposes it. The actors let the audience follow development of the conflict to a climax and a resolution. This makes a solid foundation for an interesting improvisation.

In order for action to avoid becoming antiseptic, create obstacles for the character. Obstacles which will make the role interesting and imaginative. All signs of life need not be removed from the scene. Doors may stick, telephone cords can get tangled and drinks spill.

Some shows have more than their share of problems the actors must contend with. For instance, the night Steve Allen and wife Jane Meadows opened in the Los Angeles Civic Light Opera's *Cinderella* at the Pantages Theater, Hollywood, they had to cope with an indecisive curtain, a misbehaving magic wand, miscued lights, a mistimed special effect and crying babies in the audience. It was rough, but they handled it. They incorporated taking care of each conflict as part of the action. They did not isolate it. Subtlety was the key word.

In the Broadway play *Prelude to a Kiss*, a piece of lettuce escaped from the star's plate and fell to the stage during a dinner scene. He picked it up and placed it on the table with no break in the conversation, thus relieving the audience of worrying about it.

If the actor encounters a "real" conflict on-stage — an accident — he needs to "legalize" the mishap. Incorporate it into the scene. Do not try to overlook it. Do not break. Do not step out of character. Creativeness on-stage involves concentration in the presence of distraction. The actor must use energy to control his attention in spite of the pressure of distraction. "The show must go on. . ."

Of course, it doesn't always happen that way. There have been some egregious breaks in dramatic comportment. In the Broadway show *Grotesque Love Songs*, Sally Kirkland, a former Oscar nominee, "went up" on her lines. In other words, she suddenly forgot them. She turned her back to the audience and said, "I'm going to do something I've never done before — stop and start all over again." And she walked off. The audience was stunned, and Ms. Kirkland was dismissed.

Actor Evan Handler also walked off-stage during *I Hate Hamlet* on Broadway after co-star Nicol Williamson told him in front of the audience, "Put some life into it; use your head," then hit him with a sword during a dueling scene. An understudy finished for him. Handler, although unhurt, quit the role.

In neither case would the audience have been so disturbed had the actor remained on-stage and carried on.

Assignment

A one-minute scene in which your ongoing character bids good-bye. (Good-byes can be a form of inner conflict. They can be bittersweet, where an ending is also seen as a beginning.)

IMPROV EXERCISES

Status

WHAT: Conflict between:

WHO: High, middle and low status. (Chosen at random from cards supplied by instructor.)

WHERE: Left up to the actors.

Each group announces who characters are. Examples:

Store manager, clerk and customer.

Publisher, editor and reporter.

Head of state, prime minister and subject.

Producer, director and star.

Student shuffle.

Hello and Good-bye

WHAT (conflict): Admitted, then rejected.

WHO: Suggested by instructor.

WHERE: Suggested by instructor.

Each group announces description of improv. Examples:

Country club gathering. New members' ancestors did not come over on the Mayflower.

A dance troupe. New member has a tattoo under the tutu.

A swim club. New member has four toes.

Student shuffle.

Losers Weepers

WHAT (conflict): Something is lost.

WHO: Suggested by instructor or audience.

WHERE: Suggested by instructor or audience.

Each group announces title of improv. Examples of losses: Virginity, false teeth, a will.

Student shuffle.

ASSESSMENT

What did you learn today?

PREVIEW OF NEXT CHAPTER

Theme of exploration

Poetry to performance.

Assignment

A short poem written about yourself. Your personality, your dreams, remembrances, your acting or part of your body.

Chapter 16
POETRY TO PERFORMANCE

LECTURE NOTES

Poetry is raw emotion, using imagery to communicate. Poetry gains meaning when spoken. Oral interpretation of poetry requires the actor to convey the meaning of poetry and prose. Vocal expression, tone and movement are the tools to transmit thoughts, ideas, characters and emotion. Poetry is a form of body language. The poem needs to be treated like a speech in a play. Decide where it is taking place and who the character is, and put that character in a situation. Choose an overall action and break it down into smaller actions, using pacing — fast and slow — and pauses for dramatic effect. The choices can enhance, destroy or comment on the sense of the poem. Think about the rhythm in which the poem was written. Try not to totally control the material. Let it flow.

The use of the image in acting is the stage equivalent of imagism in poetry. For instance, think of the institution of marriage. An essayist could write a long analysis on this subject. But the poet Carl Sandberg, using imagery, said, "Wedlock is padlock."

Assignment

A short poem written about yourself — your personality, dreams, remembrances, acting or part of your body.

POETRY ON-STAGE

Some of the instructor-selected poems can be read singly, but most of them require collaborative interpretations. The poems are assigned, and five or ten minutes are allowed for preparation. When acting out a poem, emotion, tone and movement are emphasized, along with projection and pacing.

MATERIAL

Shakespeare can be used, especially his "All the World's a Stage." Limericks, Ogden Nash's *Tableau at Twilight* and Lewis Carroll's *Jabberwocky* add fun. *The Spider and the Fly* by Mary Howitt is good melodrama. For heavy drama, there is Edgar Allen Poe's *The Raven.*

METHODS

— The stanzas are generally divided among the actors in groups of three or four.

— Some poems are enhanced by supplying "a Greek chorus" to add emphasis and act as a binder.

— Other enhancements include accompanying sounds, instruments (supplied by instructor), movement and pantomime.

— Half masks (supplied by instructor) can be utilized for great effects.

— It is often useful to read a poem twice, first without accompaniment, then adding the "special effects."

ASSESSMENT

What did you learn today?

PREVIEW OF NEXT CHAPTER

Theme of exploration

Commedia dell'Arte (comedy of art or skill). Broad comedy behind half masks. Not crude burlesque or slapstick — no knocking down, banana peels or sexual innuendoes, but clever, often compassionate comedy bits called *lazzi* (pronounced "lot-see").

Assignment

From behind a half mask (supplied by instructor), a one-minute scene involving exaggerated emotion and body language. Use pantomime, dialog, props and costume pieces.

You may title your lazzi.

A classic lazzi involves an actor with a fly swatter. He enters stage, swatting at a fly and missing twice. On the third try, he smashes the pesky creature. He pantomimes picking it up, slowly pulling off the wings, then starts to eat the remains. He stops and offers it to members of the audience, who refuse with disgust. He finally swallows it, signaling his pleasure with murmurs and smacking sounds, licking his lips and rubbing his stomach. He exits, joyfully swatting at other flies.

Chapter 17
COMMEDIA DELL'ARTE
(Comedy of Skill; literally Comedy of Art)

LECTURE NOTES

Commedia dell'Arte has been called "the sitcom of the Renaissance." It was theatre stripped down to its basic elements. The Commedia was developed by actors who toured rural Italy during the 16th century. Troupes of performers would use stock characters and plots and turn them into fabulous feats of comedy by filling a story with standard routines called lazzi. These comic bits were pinned up somewhere in the wings. Thus emerged the expression "winging it," meaning to improvise.

The actors would take the basic Commedia dell'Arte plot and characters such as Harlequin, Punchinello or Pantalone and add their own gags, tricks and stunts. The plays were most often improvisations based on long-established scenarios; the artistry lay in the wit and physicality of the players. There was no message, only entertainment and laughter. The actors performed without lavish costumes, lighting, instruments or sets. The show included just the actors, a bare stage and the audience.

Commedia left behind no scripts. It cannot be studied as literature like Shakespeare and Molière, who were greatly influenced by Commedia. Although no literature exists, there is evidence of masks. In this uniquely theatrical form, weirdly transforming half masks were used to produce larger-than-life, but utterly realistic, caricatures and walking social commentaries. Masks seem to have magical powers for producing physical comedy. Masks allow the actor to attempt impossible gestures. They turn the whole body into a larger mask. For instance, Charlie Chaplin's tramp was a mask. His character came from the clothes and the make-up — a change of appearance rather than an intellectual process. With the mask, the actor can hide in plain sight, using swiftness and simplicity as the key words.

The difference between burlesque (slapstick) and Commedia is crudeness vs. cleverness. There is no knocking down, banana peels or sexual innuendos.

Commedia is still entertaining today in the compassionate and zany characterizations of artists like Sid Caesar and Imogene Coca, Robin Williams, Red Skelton, Jonathon Winters, Lily Tomlin, Billy Crystal and Bill Irwin, among others.

Commedia was alive in Chaplin as well as Buster Keaton's great stone face and in the shenanigans of Laurel and Hardy and Jackie Gleason.

Commedia does not always have to be funny. It can be tender, moving and with pathos. For example, clown Emmett Kelly's description of his lazzi: "I am a sad, ragged little guy who is very serious about everything he attempts — no matter how futile or how foolish it appears to be. I am the hobo who found out the hard way that the deck is stacked, the dice 'frozen,' the race fixed and the wheel crooked, but there is always present that one tiny forelorn spark of hope still glimmering in his soul, which makes him keep trying."

Assignment

From behind a half mask (supplied by instructor), a one-minute lazzi involving exaggerated emotion and body language. Use pantomime, dialog, props and costume pieces. You may title your lazzi.

IMPROV EXERCISES

Build a Lazzi

WHAT (conflict): Wearing half masks, each small group of students (perhaps three or four) perform a lazzi based on an off-the-wall subject drawn from a large card selected at random such as:

Foreign encounter   Glue

Showoff	Spaghetti
Noise	Reunion
Ants	Gum
Applesauce	Trash
Money	News

WHO: Left up to the students.

WHERE: Left up to the students.

The cards are displayed as titles for lazzis.

Student shuffle.

Outrageous Assumption

Two half-masked actors enter stage from opposite sides. The first makes an outrageous assumption concerning the other, such as, "I hear you had a sex change." The second actor "goes with the flow," or the scene fails.

Student shuffle.

ASSESSMENT

What did you learn today?

PREVIEW OF NEXT CHAPTER

Theme of exploration

Familiarization with characters being assigned by instructor for a final performance: "The Remarriage of Deedee and Duke," a wild happening involving the whole class and employing all facets of improv learned to date. There will not be an actual rehearsal of the "wedding" itself, or it would not be an improv.

Assignment

A one-minute introduction of your "wedding" character, including walk, body language, voice, costume pieces, props, etc. Build your character and explore your relationship with others in the wedding party. Be ready to extemporize, utilizing what you have experienced in these classes about ensemble acting and other facets of performance art. Know your characters' traits well, whether the audience ever senses them or not.

Each student is given a brief outline for his character development as seen in the following chapter.

Chapter 18

WEDDING IMPROV CHARACTER DEVELOPMENT

Note: On the following pages are individual character descriptions with stage directions that may be copied and used by each student participating in the Wedding Improv. The Bridesmaid and Usher sheets may be used for one or as many characters as class size allows.

Bride: Dee Dee

Very Bronx and sulky. Wanna-be respectable.
Previously married to Duke. Has since mar-
ried and divorced a second hubby.

During the wedding: Enters on arm of sleazy uncle. Banters
throughout with family sitting in front row. Sits on-stage
for actual ceremony. Gives speech during wedding vowing
determination to stick it out this time. Like everyone else,
reacts when her ex-hubby enters late and sits with guests.

At the reception: Dee Dee yells at bridesmaids to form for
group picture. At head table, set up on-stage, is mushy with
Duke. Drinks, dances, gets romantic with Duke's brother,
resists advances by father-in-law. Joins in dollar dance. Her
ex cuts in and is ejected. She, like everyone else, enters the
food fight (using real bread). She cuts wedding cake, but
pushes some into Duke's face for flirting with bridesmaids.
Sits slouched in chair on dance floor as Duke gives speech
of love. Still angry, she throws her bouquet violently at one
of the flirtees and knocks over presents as they exit, arguing
loudly.

Fill in. Improvise.

Mother of the Bride

Loud, flashy, sleazy. Like her daughter, is very Bronx. Wanna-be respectable. Dressed in black because she opposes the remarriage.

During the wedding: Led down the aisle by an usher, she talks loudly all the way. Reacts to bride's twin sister, grandmother and cousin recently out of sanitarium. Spots her sister's child, a nun, in new religious outfit. Makes her turn around to view it at all angles. Remarks about flowers, decorating, altar . . . anything. Reacts to groom's parents across the aisle. Treats daughter as a little girl. Cries when she comes down the aisle and cries when she leaves.

At the reception: Reacts to everything. Cries over dead husband. Shows his picture around. Calms nun down over jazzy music. Sits drinking and singing. Dances. Horrified when things start going wrong — drunkenness, people falling down, food fight, etc. Cries loudly when couple leaves.

Fill in. Improvise.

Twin Sister of Bride

Wears an eye patch. Is angry because she was not chosen as the maid of honor or a brides- maid.

During the wedding: Is led down the aisle to front row. Reacts to cousins, one a newly ordained nun and the other recently out of a mental home. Gives scathing wedding speech.

At the reception: Uptight all the way as she sits, drinks and dances. In food fight, throws bread at the bride. Tries to catch the bouquet.

Fill in. Improvise.

Grandmother of the Bride

Hard of hearing.

During the wedding: Ushered in and seated in front row. Takes out knitting. Reacts to bride's mother (her daughter), bride's twin sister, cousin from mental home and cousin who is a nun. Reacts to ceremony, interrupting often. "I can't hear! What'd he say?"

At the reception: Eats, drinks, dances and sings. Reacts to everything. Falls down on floor to get attention. Tries to catch the bouquet.

Fill in. Improvise.

Bride's Cousin

May be a man or a woman. Just out of mental ward. Quite spacey. Wears a wild hat.

During the wedding: Ushered in and seated in front row. Reacts to rest of family, especially the nun. Argues when asked to remove hat. Leaves ceremony in the middle, saying, "I have to go to the bathroom."

At the reception: Wanders aimlessly around room with vacant smile, selling grocery coupons.

Fill in. Improvise.

Cousin of the Bride

Newly ordained nun.

During the wedding: Ushered into front row. Reacts to sermon throughout. Glows. Leads guests in song when called upon by vicar.

At the reception: Objects to piano player's jazzy tunes. Begins drinking. Later dances to music. Tries to catch the bouquet.

Fill in. Improvise.

Former Husband of Bride

The sort of guy who would show up at his ex-wife's wedding.

During the wedding: Enters alone and late. Sits in chair halfway back. Reacts to wedding.

At the reception: Drinks. At dollar dance, drunkenly tries to cut in on Dee Dee. Makes a scene and is ejected by ushers.

Fill in. Improvise.

Groom: Duke

*Very sulky, loud, flashy, wanna-be respecta-
ble. Previously married to Dee Dee. Perhaps
their marriage broke up because of his gambling.*

During the wedding: Enters from side. Banters with his
family in front row and his brother, the best man. Sits on-
stage for ceremony. He gives speech, vowing to give up
gambling for her sake.

At the reception: During group picture, pinches the behind
of pregnant maid of honor. Becomes mushy with Dee Dee
at head table. Starts food fight. Drinks, dances, flirts with
one or two of the bridesmaids. Dollar dance. Cutting of wedding cake, gets cake in the face. Gives speech of eternal love
while Dee Dee slouches in chair. They exit together, loudly
arguing.

Fill in. Improvise.

Mother of the Groom

Sleazy, loud, wanna-be respectable.

During the wedding: Led down the aisle by husband, talking loudly. Reacts to grandmother and groom's sister, stripper Kitty Litter. Reacts to bride's mother across the aisle. Not friendly. Relationship with own husband unhappy. Treats groom as little boy. Talks with him while waiting for service to start. Reacts to bride and groom walking back down the aisle.

At the reception: Dances, drinks, sings. Reacts to husband trying to make out with bride. Reacts when things start going wrong. Reacts when couple leaves.

Fill in. Improvise.

Father of the Groom

Sleazy, loud, wanna-be respectable. Dressed in tux and snakeskin shoes. Wears big, flashy rings.

During the wedding: Leads wife down the aisle. Reacts to grandmother and groom's sister (his daughter), stripper Kitty Litter. Reacts to bride's parents. Has eyes for bride.

At the reception: Dances, drinks, sings, tries to make out with bride, joins in food fight. Tries to make out with bridesmaid. Later slips slowly, slowly out of chair to the floor.

Fill in. Improvise.

Best Man

Brother of the groom.

During the wedding: Ushers, seating families in front row, bride's on the left, groom's on the right. After ushering, joins groom. Makes wedding speech about groom. Has eyes for bride.

At the reception: Drinks, dances, sings. Joins in food fight. Makes a move on the bride.

Fill in. Improvise.

Grandmother of the Groom

Myopic and walks with cane.

During the wedding: Ushered in and seated in front row. Reacts to sister of groom, stripper Kitty Litter. Reacts to groom's mother and father and entire ceremony.

At the reception: Eats, drinks and sings. Tries to catch the bouquet.

Fill in. Improvise.

Groom's Sister

Stripper Kitty Litter.

During the wedding: Ushered in and seated in front row. Reacts to bride's family, her own grandmother, mother and father. Reacts to ceremony. Takes a sexy liking to vicar.

At the reception: Eats, drinks, sings and dances. Finally starts stripping to jazzy music and is pulled away by ushers. Tries to catch the bouquet.

Fill in. Improvise.

Maid of Honor

Unmarried, eight and a half months pregnant. Dressed just short of tacky. Chews gum.

During the wedding: Enters by herself. Sits on-stage. Stares in disbelief and curiosity at nun. Turns head in unison with bridesmaids from vicar to nun.

At the reception: Eats, drinks, takes off shoes, dances, sings. Joins in food fight. Tries to catch the bouquet.

Fill in. Improvise.

Bridesmaid

Wears same color as other bridesmaids, but tackily dressed. Chews gum.

During the wedding: Enters by herself and sits on-stage. Stares in disbelief and curiosity at nun. Turns head from vicar to nun in unison with other bridesmaids.

At the reception: Drinks, dances, sings. Joins in food fight. Makes out with male members of audience. Tries to catch the bouquet.

Fill in. Improvise.

Vicar

Not your run-of-the-mill cleric. Wears baseball cap, carries clipboard.

During the wedding: First to enter from side. Removes baseball cap, places it and clipboard on lectern. Addresses guests and gives brief exposition. "We welcome you to the remarriage of Dee Dee and Duke," etc. Announces bingo next week with TV and VCRs as prizes. Announces speeches from bride's sister, groom's brother and bride and groom. Invites nun to sing. Leaves lectern and stands behind couple and asks, "Who shall object to this wedding?" etc.

At the reception: Proceeds to drink and interact with wedding party. Slowly becomes tipsy. Can't find table. Asks guests for directions.

Fill in. Improvise.

Wedding Coordinator

Officious, sharp-tongued. All-around nasty.

At the reception: In full charge of all elements. Oversees caterers, piano player, photographers. Flutters about during reception.

Fill in. Improvise.

Caterer

May be man or woman.

At the reception: Serves champagne (in pantomime), food (real bread), and cake (make-believe). Brings in fly swatter to swat an imaginary fly on the cake. Sips a little.

Fill in. Improvise.

Usher

Friend of groom.

During the wedding: Asks guests and family members, "Are you friends of the bride or the groom?" Seats them accordingly (left side for bride, right for groom). Seats family in front row. Joins groom and best man on-stage.

At the reception: Drinks, dances, makes out. Joins in food fight.

Fill in. Improvise.

Photographer

A nerd.

During the wedding: Takes pictures with prop camera.

At the reception: Clicks everything. Stays in the middle of the action. Circles bride and groom. Argues with wedding coordinator.

Fill in. Improvise.

Piano Player

Perhaps wears a Harpo Marx-style wig.

During the wedding: Plays wedding music throughout.

At the reception: Plays jazz. Has at least one altercation with the nun, who thinks his music obscene (until she gets tipsy and begins to enjoy it). Plays a risqué number, which prompts Kitty Litter to begin stripping. She is removed before too much is.

Fill in. Improvise.

Chapter 19
THE BIG FINISH

After a series of improv workshops employing the various exercises already discussed, it can be fun and satisfying for the actors to stage a full-cast "show." Instant improv, in which one or just a few students perform, obviously is not written or rehearsed. It would not be improv. For a large group, however, some sort of framework is necessary in order to prevent a chaotic mob scene in which everyone is milling about and trying to talk over each other.

It was estimated that about 25 percent of the highly successful Broadway show *Tony n' Tina's Wedding* was scripted, enabling the performers to improvise through most of their hilarious wedding and reception scenes that drew members of the audience (the "guests") into the action.

Other types of gatherings lend themselves to large-cast improv shows and suggested bare-bones scripting for some of them are presented in a following chapter titled "More Ideas." They are a trial, a clown's funeral and a 50-year high school reunion.

"The Remarriage of Dee Dee and Duke"

LECTURE NOTES

A students' improvisational spoof of the hit New York and Los Angeles show *Tony n' Tina's Wedding* served as the semester "final" for Students on Stage. Acquaintances, relatives and members of the public were invited to this outlandish piece of participatory theatre. At the remarriage of Dee Dee and Duke, guests were *more* than part of the audience, they were friends of the family. Even if the audience was just being themselves, they were in the act. They were playing.

Character development: This is *definitely* an ensemble

show. Within that ensemble, however, come wildly individual characterizations. But there is a unity of purpose, the thrill of a group of actors merging into a unified — if somewhat shapeless — show and being committed to a joint concept. They are not numerous individuals working separately. The key words are *listen* and *react*. It is the immediacy that is important.

Outwardly, the characters are dressed like a million dollars. Inwardly, they are dressed like 50 dollars. Bridesmaids could wear red, for instance, and the unhappy mother of the bride, black. Although the frame is set, the action is not, which leads to a wide range of connections: Funny, sweet, sly, confrontational and strange. A wedding brings out strong emotions as the characters move and improvise individually with each other and members of the audience, talking, reacting and playing off them.

Stay in character at all times

Know your character so well that you cannot be fazed. Concentrate on diction, clarity and detail of character. Perhaps the bridal party consists of sulky former spouses remarrying, sleazy in-laws, an inebriated priest, a singing nun, nerdy photographers, a stripper cousin, gum-chewing bridesmaids, a pregnant maid of honor, morose ex-boyfriend, an 87-year-old grandmother giving away grocery coupons and ushers selling hot VCRs.

Assignment

A one-minute introduction of your wedding character with your walk, body language, voice, costume pieces, props, etc.

CHARACTER REHEARSAL IN ENSEMBLE SCENES

Sample combinations

— Bride, groom and bride's grandmother.
— Bride's mother and vicar.

— Bride's twin sister, ditzy cousin and nun cousin.

— Maid of honor and two bridesmaids.

— Groom's mother, father, grandmother and stripper cousin.

— Groom's brother and two lecherous cousins.

— Wedding coordinator, photographers and caterers.

This gives students an advance chance to "play off" each other as their assigned characters.

Instructor hands out *Vague, Unrehearsed Order of Events*, which students go over together with basic blocking of major action. This is only a suggested framework to ensure a relatively unchaotic performance. No dialog is rehearsed.

VAGUE, UNREHEARSED ORDER OF EVENTS

The Wedding

The stage is set with lectern and several chairs. Actor-guests and the audience are seated on rows of chairs as though in a chapel or church.

Pianist enters and plays softly. *Wedding Coordinator* officiates at door where fake presents are stacked.

Ushers escort families and guests to seats, asking them whether they are friends of the bride or groom and seating them accordingly.

Vicar enters. Inspects set-up, smiles, exits.

Nun enters, prays, teaches song to guests, takes seat.

Vicar reenters; stands beaming at crowd.

Groom and *Best Man* enter from side. *Ushers* join them.

Wedding March. *Bridesmaids* and *Maid of Honor* come down center aisle and sit on-stage. *Bride* enters on arm of *Uncle*.

Bride and *Groom* sit facing each other on-stage.

Best Man and *Ushers* sit on-stage.

Vicar gives exposition speech (identifying the wedding party) and folksy or hip lecture; announces BINGO prizes.

Bride's Former Husband enters and sits center. *Vicar* acknowledges. *Others* react.

Speeches by *Sister of the Bride, Brother of the Groom,* the *Bride* and the *Groom.*

Nun leads flock in song. *Vicar:* ". . . forever hold your peace," etc. Pronounces them wed.

Bride and *Groom* exit to rear of auditorium.

Auditorium lights switched on.

Bridesmaids exit on arms of *Best Man* and *Ushers.*

Family members exit.

Guests are immediately instructed to turn their chairs toward the center of the room, leaving space for dancing in the middle. They will then be facing the action for . . . God knows what!

The Reception

The lectern is removed and replaced by a long table and chairs for the wedding party — *Newlyweds, Ushers* and *Bridesmaids.*

Pianist plays low-down jazz. *Caterers* pantomime pouring champagne from empty bottles into plastic glasses. Serve real bread. *Family members* reenter and mill around, talking with guests. *Family* and *Guests* pantomime toasts.

Wedding Coordinator calls for group photo.

Nun complains to *Pianist* about the music. *Bride's Mother* calms her down.

Family members and *Guests* sit.

Dancing begins.

Caterers pantomime pouring more champagne.

Wedding Coordinator organizes throwing of bridal bouquet.

Wedding Coordinator announces Dollar Dance and urges the guests to participate — even hands out imaginary or play money. *Bride's Former Husband* keeps cutting in. Has to be removed by *Ushers*.

Bread fight started by *Duke* from head table.

Sister Kitty Litter begins to strip. Is restrained by *Ushers*.

Vicar, after too much champagne, can't find his table.

Nun, tipsy, starts dancing alone to the music.

Caterers roll in real or fake cake on cart. Have to swat fly on cake.

Cake cutting. *Groom* feeds piece to *Bride* (pantomime).

Bride and *Groom* start arguing. Cake in face (pantomime).

Bride knocks over presents. Slouches sullenly in chair as *Groom* gives speech of eternal love.

They exit auditorium together, still arguing. Imaginary rice thrown.

SHOW TIME

A press release similar to the following could be sent to local newspapers in order to draw a crowd to *The Remarriage of Dee Dee and Duke*. Copies of the press release may also be passed out at the door.

STUDENTS ON STAGE

Students on Stage is a drama class developed and conducted through MiraCosta College, where it is under the Psychology Department as "Self-Awareness Through Dramatic Interaction."

SOS is conducted by Brie Jones, former television and stage actress now living in Carlsbad. It is held every Wednesday afternoon and is attended regularly by about 30 men and women who participate in improvisations designed to teach them the fundamentals of acting as well as to heighten self-confidence and a sense of humor. Other major aims are to break down inhibitions and to help participants know themselves.

Members of the class devise and perform extemporaneous skits to carry out the weekly assignments, such as showing how one would contend with sudden adversity, conveying a story using only gibberish or pantomime, or portraying human beings with animal characteristics.

The course has been in existence for five years. Its members range from those with no acting experience to a few who work professionally.

The Remarriage of Dee Dee and Duke, a spoof of the hit New York and Los Angeles show, *Tony n' Tina's Wedding*, serves as the semester "final" for SOS members.

Those in the cast have been assigned roles and have explored their relationships with others in the wedding party. They will then extemporize, presumably utilizing what they have learned about ensemble acting and other facets of stage performance.

Copies of the cast list seen below may also be handed out at the door.

THE REMARRIAGE OF DEE DEE AND DUKE

The Cast

Wedding Coordinator
Vicar

Bride's Family
Dee Dee
Mother
Twin Sister
Grandmother
Cousin (recent mental patient)
Cousin (newly ordained nun)
Maid of Honor
Bridesmaid
Bridesmaid
Former Husband
Uncle (may not arrive)

Groom's Family
Duke
Mother
Father
Best Man (brother)
Grandmother
Sister Kitty Litter
Usher (friend)
Usher (friend)

Photographer
Caterer
Piano Player
Freeloading Guests

Props

Chapter 20
MORE IDEAS

Useful for a final improv is any situation where groups of people meet and which provides an opportunity for them to play off each other. As noted before, some framework is necessary in large-cast improvs to prevent utter chaos.

Such as:

THE TRIAL OF GOLDILOCKS

An improv

Goldilocks is on trial for trespassing, burglary (of porridge), invasion of privacy, vagrancy, vandalism and unlawful entry. During her trial, prospective jurors are questioned closely about their feelings. Are they prejudiced against bears? Do they think all blondes are dumb bimbos? The improv can include witnesses for and against the defendant, the bears themselves and various members of the court.

A suggested cast

Defendant Goldilocks

Judge

Prosecutor

Defense Attorney

Jurors

Three Bears

Woodcutter

Animal Regulation Officer

Character Witnesses

Goldie's Mother and Grandfather

Translator who speaks bear

Policeman

An announcer could set the stage with a few words about the trial:

"Ladies and not ladies, welcome to our tale of woe. What you see before you is a courtroom in which soon will begin the trial of Goldilocks, accused of violating the home of the much-maligned bears.

"There is more to the story than you have ever heard. We have always been told only one side of the events and have no doubt come away with the impression that the Three Bears were rude and inhospitable. Now the other side of that infamous day in the woods will unfold as the Three Bears have hired a lawyer to prove that they should not be blamed for any behavior brought on by the defendant's invasion of their privacy. The bears have rights as homeowners and those rights must be respected.

"Let us be perfectly clear that the Three Bears are not on trial here. But the defense will attempt to make them so. The American Civil Liberties Union has argued that in chasing Ms. Goldilocks out of their house, the Three Bears were only following their instincts and deserve psychological treatment for their traumatic experience.

"An environmentalist has pointed out that bears are an endangered species and thus protected from humans. The Child Abuse Hot Line has weighed in with a charge of child endangerment against Goldilocks' mother for allowing her daughter to walk alone through bear-infested woods. And obviously without supplying her breakfast. If you remember, the poor little thing was famished at the sight of porridge.

"So we shall see the turn of events this trial takes and set straight once and for all the real story of the Three Bears.

"Do not be frightened by the bears, as they are domesticated, potty-trained and gentle as the rain that droppeth from heaven on the place beneath. Rather, be wary of Goldilocks and her groupies.

"I believe the proceedings are about to commence . . ."

So much for setting the tone. Jurors can decide Goldilocks' guilt or innocence based on testimony by the defendant, the bears and others. The judge may rule on admission of various bits of testimony or evidence, as in any criminal trial.

BIPPO BITES THE DUST
(A la Mary Tyler Moore's *"Chuckles the Clown" episode)*

Vague Outline

This interactive theatre improv's strength is participatory chaos through distinct characters and a narrative anchor centered around a clown's death and its effect on an extended circus "family" divided into warring factions.

Characters

Choir

Rev. Rotinhell — Funeral Director

Wife — Nellie Fly

Daughter — Allura Dawn

Snake Charmer — Clammy Jane

Musician — Drummer Willy Nilly

Elephant Trainer — Gruesome Griswold

Ghost of Bippo

Lawyer — Devil U. Say

Tight-rope Walker — Tippy Tutu

Busybody Bearded Lady — Olga Cassini

Lion Tamer — Noel Coward

Magician — Holy Smokes

Mime — Ms. Mum
Siamese Twins — Me and You
Clowns — Rusty, Dusty and Musty
Parade Pooper Scooper — Silky Dude

The scene is set with several objects of furniture bearing sale tags (i.e., *As is, $3.98*).

The service begins with singing by the choir. Funeral director enters.

"I am Reverend Rotinhell, here today to give a dignified farewell to Bippo the Clown. Although I did not know this personage, I am competent to speak about him because I studied my craft in Transylvania.

"The entire circus world mourns the passing of Bippo. He was believed to be in his early 60s. It was hard to tell when he was always wearing a rubber nose. He has long been ranked with four other great circus clowns: Otto Griebling, Felix Adler, Lou Jacobs and Emmett Kelly. He will be remembered by children and adults alike.

"They shall not soon forget Bippo's white-face make-up with its goofy smile, plum-sized nose and the tiny hat perched precariously upon his pointed head.

"We can all recall his riotous antics, including sliding around the hippodrome track on water skis and powering past spectators in a motorized bathtub.

"But his most famous act was as Mr. Fee Fi Fo with his engaging puppet, Flannel Mouth." (*REVEREND ROTINHELL pulls puppet from his coat and fits it over his hand for remainder of the eulogy.*) "And whenever Mr. Fee Fi Fo made his fanny falls, he would always pick himself up, dust himself off and say his catch phrase, 'I hurt my foo-foo!' Life is a lot like that. From time to time we all fall down and hurt our foo-foos. If only we could deal with it like Bippo.

"Bippo began in show business as the tail end of an alligator costume when he was seven and came to the attention of circus officials years later with his fully operational two-foot by three-foot car into which he managed to cram his six-foot, one-inch body, spending many minutes trying to extricate himself.

"Unfortunately, Bippo crammed himself into the tiny vehicle one too many times, and Ethel the Elephant mistakenly sat on it. Ethel had just exited from the middle ring and stopped to raise her front legs in acknowledgement of the spectators' applause while waving a tiny American flag with her trunk. Bippo died a broken man.

"Sadly, all good things come to an end. Even this funeral home is changing. It will soon become The Mortuary, a dance club.

"Let us all remember Bippo's favorite poem, *The Clown Credo*: 'A little laugh, a little chase, a little custard in your face.'

"And now, for a few individual remembrances, the first being from Bippo's beloved wife, Nellie Fly."

Goofy testimonials follow. At one point a conga line forms when drummer Willy Nilly beats out rhythm on his drums in honor of Bippo. The testimonials end with lawyer Devil U. Say's revelation that none of them get any of Bippo's money, after which the audience breaks up into interactive bedlam as the cast reacts and stalks out in high dudgeon.

A final suggestion for a group improv involves:

A REUNION

In which, for example, the graduates of the 1942 class of Aaron Burr High School come together for their 50th graduation anniversary. The head cheerleader may have become a CIA agent. Perhaps the class president is now a

Mafia figure, the ROTC commander has become an anti-military activist, a dropout is now a judge and the class secretary is an over-the-hill actress.

What if the class bimbo or tramp is now a nun? Or the spelling bee captain has become an absent-minded professor? Maybe the class snob, whose parents never begrudged her anything, is now the madam of a Nevada bordello ranch. There are all sorts of possibilities, as unlimited as the imaginations of the instructor and the students.

In the improv our actors staged, the high school mascot was the vampire bat and the school colors were black and puce, all of which made for some humorous shenanigans by a couple of aging pompom girls who led the "grads" and the audience in the school song.

Here (if you never attended Aaron Burr) are the words:

School Song
Aaron Burr High, Aaron Burr High,
We're the greatest and we know why.
We've got the moxie, we've got the juice,
So fight, fight, fight
For the black and the puce!

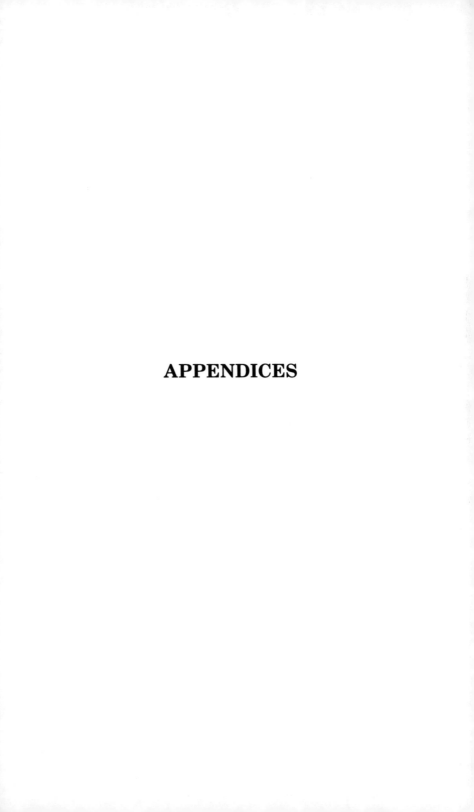

APPENDICES

I: SELF-AWARENESS
THROUGH DRAMATIC INTERACTION

Class Syllabus (Sample)

Instructor:

Subtitle   SOS: Students on Stage

Overview   Drama workshop for acting students with or without experience in the performing arts. Each participant works at *his or her own level with no comparison to other members.* In exploring dimensions of theatrical self-expression, this course will employ lecture, discussion and classroom activities to raise issues that stretch self-awareness through dramatic interaction involving imagination and creativity. Group cooperation, relation to others and self-awareness will be enhanced by speaking and performing before an audience.

Objectives   a. To have creative fun, eliminate inhibitions, sharpen acting talents, gain knowledge of self and raise self-esteem.

                    b. To practice social skills: cooperation, trust, communication and discipline.

                    c. To improve speaking ability, body language, teamwork and interaction with others.

                    d. To increase humor and self-confidence.

                    e. To heighten awareness and appreciation of theatre arts.

Standards   Students will be expected to attend class regularly and participate in assignments and activities.

Assignments   Weekly assignments will be given involving dramatic exercises.

129

Outline	Classes will include speech, body movement and off-the-wall happenings involving stage techniques, character development, improvisations, pantomime and theatre games.
Materials	Students may need various props and costume pieces.
Methods for Evaluation	a. Attendance b. Participation c. Observable growth in stage presence
Attendance	Performing class limit is 30. However, visitors and non-participants are always welcome.

II: GUIDELINES

1. *Content* of stage presentations should *not* include material that is *racist, political* or *religious.*

2. The goal is to be creative and clever, *not* raunchy.

3. Be ready in wings to follow preceding actor.

4. Set up furniture and props while instructor is evaluating preceding action.

5. Yell "S.O.S.!" after setting up furniture and props to indicate scene beginning.

6. Remain in wings until end of scene if you have exited stage.

7. Walk *behind* audience to regain your seat.

8. When there is side-coaching from the instructor (for instance, "project") do not break the fourth wall. Carry on with scene. (The fourth wall is the space through which the audience views the performance.)

9. If your presentation is too lengthy, a clicker, bell or horn will sound. If further action is needed, a rubber chicken will be thrown on-stage in lieu of a hook.

10. No food or drink allowed in the classroom.

III: OUTLINE OF CHARACTER'S HISTORY

Before you can live convincingly in the present on-stage, you must have a fully realized past. This may not show up in dialog, but use it to flesh out interpretation.

Character

Word

Profession

Image

Animal

Body Movement *(Decide what the body does first. All else follows.)*

    Walk

    Gestures

Psychological Gesture

Rhythm

Speech Pattern

Color

Costume Pieces

Props

Hobby

Gift

Social and Psychological Traits

Place of birth	Intellectual/emotional
Family	Optimist/pessimist
Education	Resilient/depressive
Work	Strong/weak
Morals	Active/passive
Friends	Habitual/risk taker
Living style	

How is character like you?

How is character unlike you?

IV: CHARACTERS CREATED FROM *OUTSIDE*

Charlie Chaplin

Developed the Little Tramp from outside-in. He chose exaggerated, non-matching costume pieces (small hat vs. oversized shoes, tight jacket vs. baggy pants). He added the mustache to make himself older and the cane as his main prop.

Laurence Olivier

Frequently brought a character to life by deciding first on a type of nose!

Peter Falk

States he evolved Colombo from outside (the rumpled raincoat, the cigar, the battered car, the sad dog and evidence carried in a paper bag).

Some of his characteristics, however, can be either inside or outside — or both (his never-seen wife and his favorite food, chili and hot dogs).

V: CHARACTERS CREATED FROM *INSIDE*

Actress Barbara Hershey in the movie *Tune in Tomorrow* invented an entire biography for her character of Julia. She pretended that her character had fled from New Orleans at 16, waiting tables in Greenwich Village, marrying first a politician and then a poet before returning home in divorced disgrace. *None of this made-up history appears in the film and little of it is even mentioned.*

"Hemingway once said, 'If you know something very well, you can leave it out and it will still be there, and if you don't know something well, you'll probably over-describe it,'" Ms. Hershey said.

Her advice is to use details as fuel for your instincts. There's a life that begins to live through you in rehearsing a role. You start speaking differently, sitting differently, having ideas in the middle of the night.

Ms. Hershey had her character Julia fool herself a lot. She's someone who thinks she's a New York sophisticate, but who's actually a deep romantic trying to protect herself. Her gum chewing, her smoking, her dark glasses are ways to cover up her failings. She hasn't admitted it, but she's coming back home with her tail between her legs.

RECOMMENDED READING

Caruso, Sandra, and Clemens, Paul. *Actor's Book of Improvsation.* New York: Penguin Books, 1992.

Hodgson, John, and Richards, Ernest. *Improvisation.* New York: Grove Weidenfield, 1987.

Johnstone, Keith. *Impro: Improvisation and the Theatre.* New York: Theatre Arts Books, 1979.

Spolin, Viola. *Improvisation for the Theater.* Illinois: Northwestern University Press, 1987.

Yakim, Moni. *Creating a Character.* New York: Back Stage Books, 1990.

ABOUT THE AUTHOR

B. (Brie) Stewart Jones academically has an M.A. in behavioral science from California State University at Dominguez Hills. Artistically, she has performed professionally on the stage since childhood in the United States and later in Europe. She financed her way through Los Angeles City College drama classes by portraying Mad Agnes and playing in olio skits at the long-running stage show, *The Drunkard.* Her television credits include, among others, several appearances on *Dragnet*, where Jack Webb became impressed with her work and paid for her wedding.

In combining the two disciplines, behavioral science and theatre arts, she has conducted workshops for all ages in dramatic interaction. Improvisation is her favorite form of acting — on stage and off.

Other books by Brie Jones as B. Stewart Jones:

#!@* On You, Mrs. Jones
Day-by-Day in an Inner-City Preschool
— *Pitman Learning, Inc.*

Hello, World!
Creative Development in Early Childhood
Through Movement and Art
— *Pitman Learning, Inc.*

Movement Themes
Topics for Early Childhood Learning
Through Creative Movement
— *Century Twenty One Pub.*

Order Form

Meriwether Publishing Ltd.
P.O. Box 7710
Colorado Springs, CO 80933
Telephone: (719) 594-4422
Website: www.meriwetherpublishing.com

Please send me the following books:

_____ **Improve With Improv! #BK-B160**   **$14.95**
by Brie Jones
A guide to improvisation and character development

_____ **Theatre Games for Young Performers #BK-B188** **$16.95**
by Maria C. Novelly
Improvisations and exercises for developing acting skills

_____ **Theatre Games and Beyond #BK-B217**   **$16.95**
by Amiel Schotz
A creative approach for performers

_____ **Acting Games — Improvisations and**   **$15.95**
Exercises #BK-B168
by Marsh Cassady
A textbook of theatre games and improvisations

_____ **Improvisation in Creative Drama #BK-B138**   **$12.95**
by Betty Keller
*A collection of improvisational exercises and sketches
for acting students*

_____ **Truth in Comedy #BK-B164**   **$16.95**
by Charna Halpern, Del Close and Kim "Howard" Johnson
Honest-to-life monologs for young actors

_____ **Everything About Theatre! #BK-B200**   **$17.95**
by Robert L. Lee
The guidebook of theatre fundamentals

These and other fine Meriwether Publishing books are available at
your local bookstore or direct from the publisher. Use the handy
order form on this page.

Name: _____

Organization name: _____

Address: _____

City: _____ State: _____

Zip: _____ Phone: _____

❑ **Check enclosed**

❑ **Visa or MasterCard #** _____

Signature: _____ *Expiration
date:* _____
(required for Visa/MasterCard orders)

Colorado residents: Please add 3% sales tax.
Shipping: Include $2.75 for the first book and 50¢ for each additional book ordered.

❑ *Please send me a copy of your complete catalog of books and plays.*